Fine Books and Book Collecting

Alan G Thomas at a Sotheby's sale 10 December 1980

FINE BOOKS AND BOOK COLLECTING

Books and Manuscripts acquired from
ALAN G. THOMAS
and described by his customers
on the occasion of his seventieth birthday

⇒∘⊙∘⇐

edited by Christopher de Hamel and
Richard A. Linenthal

James Hall
Leamington Spa 1981

Published by **James Hall (Publishing) Limited**, 2a Upper Grove Street, Leamington Spa, Warwickshire, Great Britain

© James Hall (Publishing) Limited 1981

Designed by Tom Colverson. Filmset in Palatino and Plantin by Robcroft Limited, London WC1. Printed and bound in Great Britain by Billing and Sons Limited and Kemp Hall Bindery Limited, Guildford, London, Oxford

British Library Cataloguing in Publication Data

Fine books and book collecting
   1.   Bibliography—Rare books—Festschriften
   2.   Manuscripts—Festschriften
   3.   Thomas, Alan G.
   I.   de Hamel, Christopher
   II.   Linenthal, Richard A.
   III.   Thomas, Alan G.
   090   Z1029

ISBN   0-907471-03-X

Contents

*Gregory IX, 'Fons Sapientiae': Bull for the canonisation of St Dominic, Rieti, 13 July 1234, 505x408mm
(A.G. Thomas, Catalogue 33, 1975, no.99; now in the library of W.H. Crain, Texas)*

Foreword

LAWRENCE DURRELL

It is a disadvantage to know the subject of your portrait too well: and with Alan Thomas the case is further compounded by the fact that since his early twenties he has been virtually a member of the Durrell family. I must have been twenty-two when we first met. He had already started to grasp at the first rungs of the ladder by working as a bookseller's assistant in the famous old bookshop in Bournemouth called Commin's. He lodged very modestly in Boscombe where I often spent an evening with him listening to music or talking books. Even then, working for a pittance as he was, he had still managed to start a collection which was housed in a large suitcase under his bed. It consisted of only four or five books but each one was so choice that I soon realised that he was going short of food in order to save money for this secret vice. During the course of this acquaintance among the bookshelves, which soon ripened into a warm intimacy, I asked him to lunch at the Durrell clinic — for that is how it seemed, so self-centred and so unpredictable were the inmates. My mother looked Alan up and down carefully and later confided to me in the kitchen: 'That young man needs fattening up. He's nothing but a garden rake.' But despite all her efforts, and even in later prosperous days his own, nobody has succeeded in really fattening Alan up. And happily. He has the figure of an Elizabethan courtier, and now in his old age, unlike the rest of us, has vastly increased his good looks, having added a fine abundant beard to his determined chin and sparkling blue eyes.

A career such as Alan's is shaped by a ruling passion — it is not simply a question of rising by automatic momentum as with so many people; in his case the additions were a phenomenal memory and a wonderful historic sense, coupled with that enigmatic factor, a nose, without which one cannot successfully speculate in his intricate and highly specialised field.

It was thanks to Alan's gifts that I was able to build up a small library of Elizabethan texts and reprints; I was not well off and Alan obtained some extraordinary bargains for me. This little library was my prize possession. Unhappily my brother contracted the deplorable habit of selling off my books when my back was turned, so to speak, in order to build his own zoology library. Returning from Belgrade or Athens I found my books gone; whereupon, since he himself was away on an expedition, I promptly sold off his books to punish him. Happily the buyer in each case was Alan and in this way not a book was lost. He simply housed both collections until we each returned to base, and after many an acrimonious discussion, sorted the matter out. Alan's role in all this will serve to illustrate his wide-ranging powers of affectionate diplomacy. My mother declared that whenever she felt rather despondent she was always cheered up by a little chat with him, 'because Alan is interested in everything we do'. She meant the Durrells, and I think we aroused a great deal of amused curiosity in Alan by our singular way of life which was so unlike that of our suburban neighbours. He has a number of anecdotes about this youthful period which he can be persuaded to tell late at night, and under seal, so to speak, and I am surprised that he has not descended to memoirs as yet.

My own admiration for Alan is based on the fact that he has remained always an ardent, enthusiastic student of literature, architecture, painting and poetry. Despite his eminence he is the same as he was at twenty. Money and honours mean little to him; he uses them to further his quest for more life. And it is this life-giving quality that makes him treasured by his friends among whom I am proud to number myself.

Introduction

CHRISTOPHER de HAMEL and RICHARD A. LINENTHAL

ALAN G. THOMAS reaches the age of seventy on 19 October 1981. He has been an antiquarian bookseller since 1927. This volume of essays is presented to him by a few of his friends and customers to mark this occasion, and as a tribute to him and to his long and distinguished career.

First as an assistant, and later as a proprietor and owner, Alan Thomas joined the book world in the firm of Horace G. Commin in Bournemouth.

Here, in a tall, narrow house, is housed a vast and fascinating collection of new and second-hand books. On the ground floor and in the basement all the new books glare at you somewhat balefully in their multi-coloured dust-jackets, but climb the creaking, uneven staircase to the four floors above, and you are transported into a Dickensian landscape. Here, from floor to ceiling in every room, are amassed arrays of old books. They line the walls of the narrow staircases, they surround you . . .

(Gerald Durrell, *The Picnic and Suchlike Pandemonium*, 1979).

'It was the first real bookshop I knew', writes Miss Jean Preston, now Curator of Manuscripts at Princeton, of her childhood visits to the shop, ' . . . and there was a special room with rare books and manuscripts, and sometimes one was allowed into it.'

Alan Thomas purchased the business in 1936 and, after serving as an anti-aircraft artillery sergeant during the War, began to specialise in the field of early and rare books. The first major manuscript he possessed was the Cicero, *Opera Philosophica*, illuminated in Florence in 1470 for Cardinal Janos Vitez; he bought it in the Peckover sale at Sotheby's in 1951 and it is now at Yale. In 1956 he sold the original business and the following year issued the first of his now celebrated catalogues in his own name from 7a Wimborne Road ('PLEASE NOTE: the address is 7A, NOT a number in the seventies'). By then he was well known for offering important books which seemed to him to be undervalued: text manuscripts, minor etchings by great masters, early printing, William Morris, architecture (a great personal favourite) and, later, Bibles and theology. In 1958-59, as President of the Antiquarian Booksellers' Association, he was instrumental in instigating the first Antiquarian Book Fair, establishing a pattern now known worldwide. In 1965 he moved the business to London to be nearer the salerooms, and he now operates from Chelsea. In 1967 he wrote a guide for bibliophiles, *Fine Books*, with chapters devoted to his acknowledged specialities, and, in 1975, a fuller version, *Great Books and Book Collectors*. He has written the standard bibliography of Lawrence Durrell, and a number of articles in various bibliographical journals.

The greatest achievements of any bookseller, however, are the books he can offer and the network of customers who buy them. Not only has Alan Thomas been a friend of major institutional libraries and of private collectors, but he has endeavoured to offer interesting books to poor students as well, and we ourselves (whose own careers began with schoolboy purchases from him) have heard time after time, in the course of assembling this volume, of his help to collectors of all kinds.

The thirty-three articles in this volume are all by customers of Alan Thomas, each giving an account of books acquired from him. Every book described here has passed through his hands. Some of the contributions are by the curators of the world's greatest libraries while others are by private collectors to whom one small purchase from him has opened up a new world of bibliophily. The articles refer to other collectors too, from the octogenarian Guildford housewife who took her manuscripts on holidays, to the eccentric, little-washed, cloth-capped amateur incunabulist whose obituary Alan Thomas wrote for *The Times* in July 1978. The books described include one of the most important finds for the study of early English printing — the Book of St Albans marked up for Wynkyn de Worde's edition of 1496 — and some which are minor items in themselves but selected for the present volume by their owners. Alan Thomas's catalogues (like the huge bookshop in the old Bournemouth days) include books from all ends of the market; this Festschrift is like a retrospective catalogue, selected by the buyers rather than by the bookseller. It includes references to Alan Thomas's own enthusiasms: to monastic ruins, medieval brasses, the courts of Renaissance Italy, cats called after early printers, Blake, and much else. Its subjects extend from an eleventh-century Pontifical, probably created for Besançon Cathedral, to a binding made for Alan Thomas's own copy of this volume. It is hoped that the articles together will tell something about the bookseller and his market, and that they will provide variety in the context of one man's contribution to the collecting and appreciation of fine books. We congratulate Alan Thomas and offer our best wishes on his birthday, and we all look forward to his hundredth catalogue which he has calculated will coincide with his hundredth birthday.

Acknowledgements
Photographs are reproduced here by kind permission of the owners

'He that stelles thes boke he Shal be hanked upon
on hoke Behend the kechen dor' (inscription in a
fifteenth-century English Book of Hours, formerly
A.G. Thomas Catalogue 12, 1963, no.15, and later
in the collection of Mrs J. O'Donnell)

Pontifical of Hugues de Salins, Besançon mid-eleventh century, and the Phillipps Sales

ANTHONY HOBSON

[Bibliothèque Municipale, Besançon]

—Lot 2345. May I say £200 to start this lot?
—Yes, sir.

An exchange on these lines between myself as auctioneer and Alan Thomas was a regular feature of the thirty-one Phillipps sales of the new series. Alan's constant support—I think he missed only one sale, that of the Americana in New York in 1969—was an invariable source of comfort to me during that immense and often difficult dispersal. He bought lot 17 in the first sale in 1965—a double vellum leaf of an account-book of John, Duke of Bedford (the owner of the Bedford Hours and Psalter)—and he was still buying at the end of the last sale of manuscripts in 1977, when lot 5136, a collection of letters and documents concerning Switzerland, was knocked down to him.

When, in 1965, the Robinson Trustees invited me to take charge of selling the remainder of the Phillipps Collection and I was shown the bank vault full of medieval manuscripts and the discreetly anonymous late Victorian house in Park Road, Barnet, every room of which contained shelves from floor to ceiling simply stuffed with later manuscripts and printed books, two things were clear to me. The first, naturally, was that here was a task that would take years to complete; an impression reinforced by the discovery that gaps on the shelves made by the early sales had a tendency mysteriously to fill up by the time of my next visit to Barnet. The second was that the collection was different in kind from the usual autograph letters and illuminated Books of Hours that formed the conventional staples of Sotheby sales. It would be necessary to find new buyers or to develop a new sensibility among existing ones if the massive array was to be absorbed.

Tim Munby's magnificent biography had, of course, already made Sir Thomas Phillipps a familiar figure, but one could not work for so long among his collection without further insights into his character. It became obvious that at times he can have had little idea of what he was buying. A bookseller's note prefaces Phillipps MS 12427, a manuscript of 1810 on Javanese tree-bark paper, 'The Javanese being one of the *least* known languages,

much time and labour would be required only to make out the nature of this considerable work', and there is no sign that the Baronet knew any more about it than his supplier. Similarly he seems never to have realised that he owned three out of the four extant manuscripts of a fifteenth-century allegorical work, *Le chemin de paradis*, by Jean Germain, Bishop of Châlon-sur-Saône; each copy was differently described on different pages of his printed catalogue. On the other hand he possessed an undoubted flair for works of real importance, even though undistinguished in appearance or written in a strange language. How else can one explain his ownership of a volume in Croat containing eleven unpublished poems by Marko Marulić, or the earliest and best manuscript of the Malay epic, *The Ballad of the Macassar War?* Every Phillipps manuscript was liable to have some point of interest about it.

I need not have felt any anxiety lest Alan's sensibilities should fail to match the diversity of the collection. As the sales progressed it became clear that his interests and sympathies were by no means trammelled by conventional views of what constituted a fine book. Indeed, they ranged as widely as the Baronet's own. He bought works not merely in French, Italian, Spanish, Latin and Greek, but also in Hebrew, Armenian, Coptic, Ethiopian, Syriac and Russian. At sales of English historical documents or of medieval illuminated manuscripts he had, of course, to face stiff competition. But on other occasions, when the offerings were more esoteric, he was able to make a killing. In 1966 he bought twenty-five out of sixty-one lots of Italian topography and local history. Two years later twenty Arabic and Persian manuscripts fell to him, including an illustrated copy of Qazwīnī's *Marvels of Creation*. Then, at a sale of Italian seventeenth-century manuscripts in 1975, he acquired an astonishing total of ninety-five out of 142 lots. All these purchases have since been gratefully welcomed by university librarians or other public or private collectors.

A few of Alan's purchases stand out in my memory. One, the second earliest manuscript of the

atq; subdiaconi ornent se cū reliquo clero · induen
tes sollēpnia uestimta · & diacom idalmaticis · atq;
subdiconi albis seriers · & stent inordine suo singuli
inyecctu · expectantes usq; dū uenit domn' eps cū p
cessione plenaria admissa · sic indieb; sollēpnib; cc̄ ·
uii · diacomb; & totide subdiaconib; · & ctro feriaris
& duob; turribulis cum incenso Cantor aut kesolestati
ut iussu fuerit · incipiant intromtu admissa · Nor
autem glari · Inipsa die iicincentit glā adintroitu ·
sedsep post psalmū reppetunt officiū h ifsq; ue
nit domn' archieps · ante altare accinct' pallio · &
incipiat excelsa uoce · Gloria inexcelsis deo ·
Et interra pax hominib; bone uol · Quo finito ·
DICAT ORATIONEM ·

aquo & iudas reat' sui
pena · & confessionis sue
latro pmiu supsit · con

cede

Charter from St Bertin 1306

PETER RAES

Charlottenlund, Denmark

One of the pleasures of knowing Alan Thomas is the way in which his experience and sense of values illuminate the art of collecting. At times he will advise against squandering resources on books of lesser quality, while at others he will recommend the acquisition of, say, an imperfect or well-worn volume because of some special quality of content, illustration, history, or association. An observation he made to me some years ago still comes to mind every time I open a much used and incomplete Wittenberg church bible of 1576: 'You know, if that book had been cleaner and complete it would probably have been bought by a wealthy library; but now you've got it, and no one can say that the sixty or so engravings, each of them a little work of art four hundred years old, are expensive at under a pound each.' I have often blessed my good fortune at having such a mentor.

Someone else who owed Alan Thomas a great deal, for opening up a new life in her later years, was my mother, Mrs O'Donnell of Guildford. Warming to his enthusiasm and to his scrupulously fair judgement, she began to explore the rather specialised field of Calendars in Books of Hours in the late 1950s, a time when prices and supplies were still possible for the smaller collector. Books of Hours led once in a while, and not unnaturally, to monastic documents. Here again Alan Thomas could provide many fascinating manuscripts to choose from, one of which gave particular pleasure to several people on both sides of the Channel: this was a copy of the charter which belonged to the Abbey of St Bertin at St Omer. Dated 13 April 1306, and written in a large liturgical hand with red and blue initials, it retains part of the wooden fillet with which it was hung on the cloister wall. The document grants special privileges to members of the Confraternity of the Charity of St Bertin who

---

[continued from page 2]

Grand Logothete, Georgios Acropolites's chronicle of the Nicaean Empire, is now in the British Library (Additional MS 59864). Another, Niccolò Borghese's life of St Catherine of Siena, the author's copy, was completed in 1500, only four days before his death at the hands of hired bravos, and was used by Giovanni Tacuino for the edition printed in Venice the following year. The illuminated title-page of the manuscript was reinterpreted by a Venetian woodcutter in the printed book; one of the rare cases where the original design for a Renaissance woodcut has survived and been identified.

Most remarkable of all, however, was the mid-eleventh-century Pontifical of Hugues de Salins, Archbishop of Besançon, containing, in Andreas Mayor's words, 'a long and detailed description of the processional liturgy used in Besançon for the major feasts from the Purification to the Ascension'. The manuscript had been studied by the Maurist Edmond Martène before 1700, but, although recorded by Montfaucon in 1739 and rebound for a nineteenth-century owner, the historian Amans Alexis Monteil, apparently by no one else since.

Besançon was anxious to acquire the book but could not raise the money in time, and Alan was the buyer at the eighth medieval sale of the new series in 1973 (lot 578). A year later I happened to spend some days in Besançon examining Cardinal Granvelle's books. I found that the Bibliothèque Municipale was still interested and put them in touch with Alan, with the happy result that the Pontifical has now returned to the place where it was written, and belongs to the library where it will be of most use to students. It was a perfect example of the services that an erudite and courageous antiquarian bookseller can render to scholarship.

Alan may not have bought more Phillipps lots than any other bookseller, though I dare say he ran his competitors fairly close, but he had the satisfaction of buying the oldest records in the collection. After the sales were over he acquired the Baronet's collection of geological specimens and fossils privately from the Trustees. It was an appropriate coda to his participation in the thirteen years of sales.

had been, or who would be, buried in the Abbey cemetery, including special Masses to be said in the Abbey, and psalms and prayers for Matins. Having disappeared after the French Revolution it was apparently bought by Sir Thomas Phillipps in the late 1820s or early 30s, when he visited St Omer, and it reappeared at Sotheby's as lot 1206 on 15 June 1970.

Seized by the wish, as so many collectors are, to follow up a promising lead, we paid St Omer a visit in the Spring of 1972. We took the charter with us and, directed by the local librarian, arrived at the door of le Chanoine Georges Coolen. We could not have been more fortunate; immediately recognizing the authenticity and significance of the document he examined it eagerly, and filled in for us the historical background of the abbey which now lay in ruins and almost totally neglected, in spite of some imposing walls and buttresses. As later correspondence and mutual enthusiasm developed the connection between my mother and le Chanoine it became clear that there was only one logical conclusion to the rather chequered life of the 1306 charter: it was sent back across the Channel, on what we hope was its last journey, to join other treasures in the magnificent collection in the town library. The local historical bulletin bore a long article on 'La Charte retrouvée', written by our friend, wherein he traces the probable course of events which brought the document back to St Omer, rejoicing that it is still possible 'de faire revenir les choses anciennes aux mêmes lieux qui les ont vu naître' (*Bulletin de la Société Académique des Antiquaires de la Morinie*, September 1972).

It is worth observing that this article by a contemporary French librarian presents the much criticized Phillipps in a most favourable light, thanks to his great generosity to the libraries of St Omer, Arras, and Lille. Likewise, it is pleasant to reflect that by hoarding large and often mixed quantities of manuscripts, Phillipps did in fact preserve for posterity much that might otherwise have disappeared. And in the history of such preservation—in this case leading from St Omer to Middle Hill, London, Guildford, and back to St Omer—the role of the antiquarian bookseller is a vital and, I like to think, satisfying link.

A *Missale pro Defunctis*
Liège, early fourteenth century

GEORGES DOGAER

Bibliothèque Royale Albert Ier, Brussels

This liturgical manuscript (Brussels, Bibliothèque Royale, MS IV 1045) is not an ordinary Missal with Calendar, Sanctoral and Temporal in the sequence of the ecclesiastical year, but a rare example of a Missal to be used for a funeral Mass, a *missale pro defunctis*. It was probably intended for the use of the abbot who is mentioned in all the rubrics of the *commendatio pro fratribus nostris* on fol.57^r. It is certainly remarkable that the Abbé Leroquais's standard work on manuscript Missals does not mention any Mass-Book of a similar character. Judging from the fact that Bishop Balderic of Liège (1008-1018) is mentioned on fol.72^r, and from fifteenth-century marks of ownership on the front flyleaf and on the inside of the back cover—'Liber monasterii Sancti Jacobi leodiensis ordinis domini benedicti in insula' and 'Liber abbatis domini Jacobi leodii in insula'—one may infer that the manuscript was written for this important Benedictine Abbey in Liège.

Each page has ten lines of text, which is most unusual in Mass-Books. The manuscript is written in a very large and angular gothic liturgical hand not unlike that used in outsized Antiphonaries and Graduals. There is only one full-page miniature in the manuscript, that at the beginning of the Canon, on fol.36^v. It represents Christ on the Cross, with St John the Evangelist on his left and the Virgin on his right. A very high and narrow pale-green Cross extends beyond the frame right over which is painted the inscription 'INRI'. Such Crosses are typical of fourteenth-century book illumination, their form gradually becoming both higher and narrower. In the traditional manner, the Cross is placed on a small pale-green hill, under which Adam is supposedly buried. The skull and bones, often lying under the Cross, are omitted here, as are the sun and moon, symbols of creation. The representation of figures is kept very sober, with just three persons. Christ is clad only in a red and light-blue perizonium which covers his knees, with several folds falling towards his feet. His left hip is turned slightly outwards, while the upper part of his body leans to the right so that he is almost S-shaped. Also characteristic are the thin arms and

slender fingers which, spread open, are nailed to the Cross. His feet, fixed with a single nail, are turned outwards. The white emaciated face inclines to the left. The Saviour's hair falls partly onto his shoulders. Above his head, which is crowned with thorns, is painted a gold halo. The blood from his five wounds is merely indicated by a few brush strokes. The Virgin, holding a book in her right hand, is turned towards Christ. A white veil covers her head, and under a mantle lined with pink and blue she wears a golden gown whose folds are accentuated with black lines and which covers her feet. St John the Evangelist is depicted in an orange-red gown under a mantle lined in pink and blue which hangs gracefully from his body. His right hand touches his chin, while his left carries a book. This depiction of St John with a hand under his chin differs from the usual representation where his hand is turned to the opposite side. The two figures each have a golden nimbus around their heads.

This symmetrical composition is painted partly against a dark blue background, partly against a pink one. Both parts are enlivened with white and red geometrical patterns, and the whole of the background is strewn with gold rosettes. The miniature is in a blue and pink frame, heightened with white and bordered with gold. The corners show the four evangelists within gold-bordered medallions. In the middle of the borders are painted the Synagogue and the Church as symbols of the Old and New Testaments. As usual, the figure of Christ crucified is repeated under the miniature.

Stylistically this Calvary bears a striking resemblance to three others: the first of them in a Ceremonial preserved in the University of Ghent (MS 233), which was copied in 1322 for St Peter's Abbey in Ghent; the second in a manuscript from the first half of the fourteenth century from St Vaast Abbey in Arras (Arras, Bibliothèque Municipale, MS 869); the third in another Canon miniature in a 1311 copy of *Somme le Roi*, preserved in Paris (Bibliothèque de l'Arsenal, MS 6329).

On the page facing the Canon miniature in BR, MS IV 1045, the *Te Igitur* begins with a large 3-line

Fol.36ᵛ, 302x220mm

An English Calendar
circa 1330

JANET BACKHOUSE

British Library

Towards the end of 1980 the British Library acquired from Alan Thomas a small Calendar with a strong East Anglian flavour, including an entry for the feast of St Guthlac, *festive in holandia*, on 11 April. It was the second occasion on which the Calendar, now BL, Additional MS 61887, had passed through Alan's hands. In the interval it had belonged to one of his favourite customers, Mrs June O'Donnell of Guildford, who died in December 1979.

The Calendar was once part of a Book of Hours written and illuminated about 1330, but the manuscript, a rare example of an Hours for English use at so early a date, was broken up a decade or more ago and individual leaves are now scattered around in a number of private collections. Two of the most important, each bearing a miniature and one including kneeling figures of the first owners, are reproduced in Maggs, *Bulletin*,7 (1973), items 3 and 4. Their style is not far removed from that seen in The Walter of Milemete treatises (Christ Church, Oxford, and BL, Additional MS 47680) which were addressed to Edward III in 1326-27. Mr Michael Michael, who has made a detailed study of the remains of the manuscript and hopes soon to publish his findings, has with some certainty identified one of the seriously damaged coats of arms on the first of the Maggs leaves as that of the Pateshulle family of Northamptonshire, no fewer than five members of which were married during a period appropriate to the original date of the book. The direct line of this family died out in 1359 with William de Pateshulle, but one of his sisters, wife

of Roger Beauchamp, was the great-great-great-grandmother of Margaret Beaufort, mother of Henry VII.

One of the most fascinating aspects of any Book of Hours is often the identification of successive owners and of the relatives and friends whose anniversaries the owners have commemorated in additions to its Calendar. By the later fifteenth century this particular manuscript had migrated into the hands of someone connected with the Hungerford family, and two anniversaries, those of Robert, Lord Hungerford (d. 18 May 1459) and of Margaret Botreaux, his wife (d. 7 February 1478), were inserted into the Calendar. The fortunes of the Hungerfords, whose principal seats were the manor of Heytesbury in south Wiltshire and Farleigh Hungerford Castle on the Wiltshire and Somerset border, were closely bound up in the political troubles of the times. The family first came into real prominence with Walter, the first baron, who fought with distinction at Agincourt, became a member of the inner circle surrounding Henry V and was Lord High Treasurer to Henry VI from 1426 to 1432. His eldest son, another Walter, died in the taking of Provins in October 1432, a fact noted in his Missal (now Tours, MS 183), which he gave to his grandson Robert shortly before he died in the summer of 1449. Another book which he owned, *Legends of the Lives of the Saints* in French (now lost), was willed by him to his daughter-in-law, Margaret Botreaux.

Walter was succeeded by the second of his sons, Margaret's husband Robert. He too served the

---

[Continued from page 6]

historiated **T** depicting a priest celebrating Mass in the presence of the Abbot holding his mitre and crozier. The two miniatures are by the same hand. It seems that the exceptionally beautiful Calvary and the initial date from the first quarter of the fourteenth century. It is extremely difficult to assign this illumination to a definite period in the miniature art of Liège, because so far very few representative examples of it are known.

During the nineteenth century BR, MS IV 1045 belonged first to William Maskell and then to A.J. Beresford-Hope. Subsequently owned by Henry Gibbs, first Lord Aldenham, whose collection was dispersed in London in 1937, it then passed to C.H. St John Hornby and was afterwards acquired by Major J.R. Abbey, whose manuscripts were sold at auction in 1975. At that sale it was bought by Mr Alan G. Thomas.

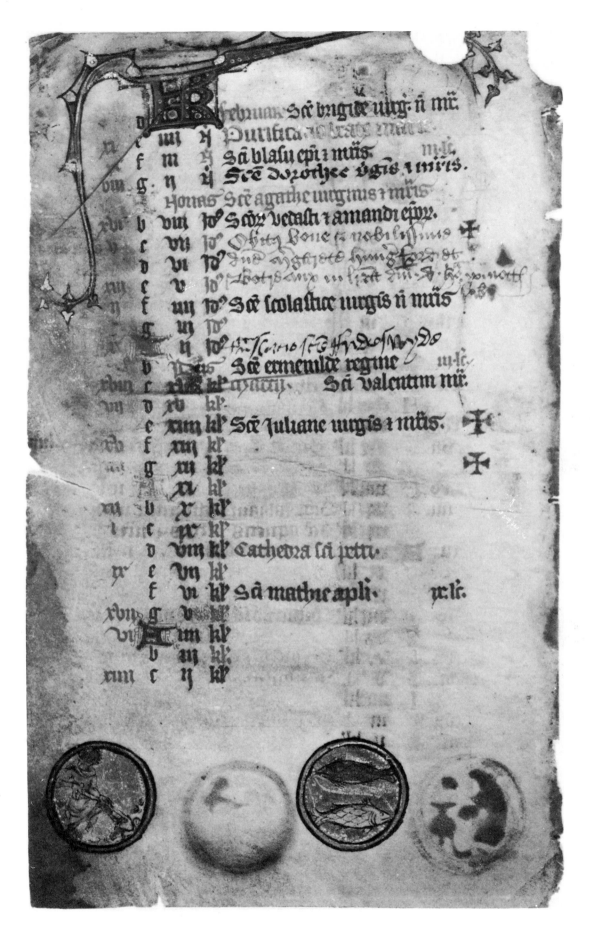

February page, fol.1ᵛ, 165x103mm

Leaf of a Bible Manuscript
France, *circa* 1330

CHRISTOPHER de HAMEL

Marden Ash

When I was about sixteen I discovered that booksellers sometimes offered fragments of medieval manuscripts and incunabula and, working through a directory of dealers, I wrote off to all the best booksellers saying that I wanted good examples but could not afford more than five pounds. I still have their replies: some are quite properly dismissive, others politely condescending, but Alan Thomas sent a chatty letter explaining that I should not be discouraged even though five pounds would not go far, and enclosing extracts from several of his catalogues and further notes about scraps I could have under my limit. Afterwards he would send details of fragments which had just come in, and endless interest was provided by leaves acquired from him. One day he offered some better fragments and, in a burst of extravagance, I bought for £12 12s. the leaf I describe here. It was the largest sum of money I had ever spent on anything and, enclosing my purchase, Alan Thomas wrote

---

[Continued from page 8]

crown in France, but he died peacefully in his bed in 1459, on the date indicated in the Calendar. Margaret's long widowhood was fraught with crisis and tragedy. Her eldest son, Robert, recipient of his grandfather's Missal, had been taken prisoner in France some years before his father's death, and Margaret found herself obliged to raise large sums of money, not only for his ransom but also for the expenses of his lordly standard of living while held in France. No sooner had he returned to England than, following his family's traditional loyalty, he became embroiled with the Lancastrian cause and was eventually beheaded at Newcastle in May 1464. His heir, Thomas Hungerford, was attainted and executed as a Lancastrian traitor early in 1469. Margaret herself was for a period confined in the nunnery at Amesbury by command of Edward IV, and while there suffered the additional misfortune of the loss of many of her personal possessions in a fire.

Following her grandson's execution, Margaret personally set about retrieving the honour and fortunes of her husband's family, buying back in 1470 portions of the lands which had been forfeited from her son, Robert. She resided at Heytesbury, Farleigh Hungerford remaining in the hands of the crown, and in 1472 fulfilled her father-in-law's wishes by finalising the foundation of Heytesbury Hospital, which is still in existence today. She also completed the family chantry in Salisbury Cathedral; its furniture and fittings are listed in the record of her activities and expenses which she annexed to her will (printed in Richard Colt Hoare's *History of Modern Wiltshire*, 1822, etc.). When she died in 1478, she entailed much of her property upon her younger grandson, Walter, who joined the standard of Henry VII at Bosworth in 1485. This Walter slew Sir Robert Brackenbury, Constable of the Tower, in single combat and was soon rewarded by the reversal of the attainder on his family and restitution of the family estates. The contemporary owner of our Calendar added a note of Richard III's death at Bosworth in the margin alongside the entry for 22 August.

The story of the Hungerfords, brought to her notice by the Calendar, fascinated Mrs O'Donnell. Although she was a collector of limited means, her imagination and enthusiasm knew no limits. She was passionately interested in antiquities and in bygones of every kind, and it was impossible to predict what treasure, in addition to the latest manuscript, was likely to appear from her bag when she made one of her very welcome appearances in the Department of Manuscripts. It was one of her particular pleasures to explore the places associated with her acquisitions. The present-day custos of Heytesbury Hospital welcomed a visit from her (and the Calendar), and my own parents had the pleasure of introducing her to Farleigh Hungerford Castle. It would have delighted her had she known that this particular item from her library would be chosen to appear amongst the birthday tributes to Alan Thomas, with whom she had so long and happy an association.

te longinquo · e de extremis terre finibz
i similitudinem aquile uolantis cui
impetu · auis linguam intelligere non
possis · gentem procaciffimam · que non
deferat sen nec misereatur paruuli · et de
uoret fetus iumentor tuorum ac fruges
terre tue donec pereas · et non relinquat e
triticum uinum oleum · armenta bou un
gregos ouuum · donec te disperdat et conterat
in cunctis urbibz tuis · et destruantur muri
tui firmi atq; sublimes · In quibz habebas
fiduciam · In omni terra tua · Obsidiberis
intra portas tuas in omni terra tua q
tabit tibi dominus deus tuus · et come
des fructum uteri tui · et carnes filiorum
tuorum et filiarum tuarum · quas dederat
tibi dominus deus tuus in anguistia et
uastitate qua opprimet te hostis tuus ·
homo delicatus in te et luxuriosus ualde
muidebit fri suo · et uxori que cubat in sinu
suo · ne det eis te carnibz filiorum suorum
quas comedet eo q nichil habeat aliud
in obsidione et penuria qua uastauerit
te inimicus tui intra omnes portas tuas ·
Tenera mulier et delicata · que super terram
ingredi non ualebat nec pedis uestigui
figere · p molliciem et teneritudinem nimi
am · Inuidebit uiro suo qui cubat in sinu
eius super filii et filie carnibz · et illuuie t
secundinar que egrediuntur de medio fe
mmum eius · et sup libis qui eadem hora u
nati sunt · Comedent eas clam p penuriam
omnium penuriam in obsidione et uasti
tate qua opprimet te inimicus tuus int
portas tuas · Nisi custodieris et feceris oi
a uerba legis huius que scripta sunt in
hoc uolumine · et timueris nomen eius glo
riosum et terribile hoc est dominum deum tuum · augm
augebit dominus plagas tuas et plagas
seminis tui plagas magnas et perseue
rantes infirmitates pessimas et perpetuas
et conuertet in te omnes afflictiones egyp
ti quas timuisti · et adherebunt tibi · Insup
et universos langores et plagas que non
sunt scripte in uolumine legis huius in
ducet dominus super te donec te conterat ·

et remanebitis pauci numero qui prius
eratis sicut astra celi pre multitudi
ne · qia non audisti uocem domini dei
tui · Et sicut ante te letatus est dominus
sup uos bn uobis faciens uosq; multi
plicans · sic letabitur disperdens uos atq;
subuertens · ut auferamini de terra ad q
ingredieris possidendam · Dispget te do
minus in omnes populos a summitate terre usq;
ad terminos eius · et seruies ibi diis alie
nis quos et tu ignoras et patres tui lignis
et lapidibz · In gentibz quoq; illis non
quiesces nec erit requies uestigio pe
dis tui · dabit enim tibi dominus ibi
cor pauidum et deficientes oculos et aiam
consumptam merore · et erit uita tua qi
pendens ante te · timebis nocte et die et no cre
des uite tue · Mane dices · Quis michi
det uespm · et uespe · quis michi det mane
pp cordis tui formidine qua terreberis · et
ppter que tuis uidebis oculis · reducet
te dominus classibus in egyptum p ui
am de qua dixit tibi ut eam amplius
non uideres · Ibi uenderis inimicis tui
in seruos et ancillas · et non erit qui ematt
Et sunt uerba federis · XXIX
Que precepit dominus moysi · ut feri
ret cum filiis israel in terra moab preter
illud fedus qd cum eis pepigit in oreb ·
Vocauitq; moyses omnem israel et dixit ad
eos · Vos uidistis uniuersa que fecit dominus
coram uobis in terra egipti pharaoni
et omnibz seruis eius · uniuerseq; terre
illius · temptationes magnas quas
uiderunt oculi tui signa illa portenta
q; ingentia · et non dedit uobis dominus
cor intelligens · et oculos uidentes · et aures
que possint audire usq; in presentem
diem · Adduxit uos xl annis per deserti ·
non sunt attrita uestimenta ura · nec cal
ciamenta pedum uestror uetustate consump
ta sunt · panem non comedistis · uinum et
siceram non bibistis · ut sciretis quia
ego sum dominus deus uester · et uenistis ad
hunc locum · Egressusq; est seon rex
esebon · et og rex basan occurrentes nob

Recto page, 295x197mm

that he hoped that I would never regret spending 'practically all I possessed'—evidently what I had told him—on the leaf I had chosen.

The leaf is from a Latin Bible on fine vellum, 295 by 197mm, double column, 46 lines per page, written in a very good gothic hand in grey-brown ink; its text is from Deuteronomy 28:49 to 30:9. The illuminated initials have full-length bar borders terminating with ivyleaves. The manuscript is certainly French and is most probably Parisian work executed in about 1320-40. I do not know whether Alan Thomas ever had other leaves from the same book, but over the years further fragments from the same manuscript have been in other dealers' catalogues: Folio Fine Art, *The Art of the Scribe* (May 1972), no.1017; C.W. Ede, *The Art of the Scribe* (May 1972), no.1; Maggs, *Bulletin*, 8 (1974), no.9, and 9 (1975), no.11; Sotheby's, 19 June 1979, part of lot 16; and The Rendells, Catalogue 146 (1979), nos 22 and 68. A bound section of six leaves was in the Lansburgh collection in Colorado (*Art Journal*, 28, 1968, pp.63-4) and is now privately owned in Spain; it includes two very fine historiated initials in the style of the Parisian illuminator Jean Pucelle. The largest group of leaves, however, appeared in the catalogues of Philip C. Duschnes, and numerous fragments, some also with historiated initials and marginal grotesques, were in Catalogues 174 (nos 8-11), 179 (nos 18-19), 187 (nos 152-3), 200 (nos 207 and 217a) and 215 (no.259). The ultimate source seems to have been Duschnes, *Medieval Miniatures and Illuminations*, Catalogue 169 (December 1964), nos 12-18, which states that many other leaves were available 'from the same incomplete manuscript Bible'. There is a striking similarity between these leaves and a slightly imperfect Bible sold at Sotheby's on 6 July 1964, lot 239 (six months before the Duschnes leaves appeared), illustrated in the catalogue with details of four initials. The proof that this was indeed the same manuscript is shown by a leaf in Laurence Witten, Catalogue 12 (1980), no.50, with a plate of the same initial which had been reproduced in the 1964 Sotheby's Catalogue, and the new owner, Dr Robert J. Parsons, has kindly sent me a photocopy of the whole leaf which confirms the identification.

A very notable feature of the volume as sold in 1964 is that it was still bound in its sixteenth-century vellum binding made up with flyleaves formed of two sheets of the Register of John Whethamstede, Abbot of St Albans (1420-40 and 1451-64). This implies that the binder had access to St Albans manuscripts shortly after the Reformation. It is, moreover, interesting that Bodleian Library, MS Douce 299 apparently has flyleaves from the same Whethamstede Register, and it has recently been shown that the Douce manuscript itself had belonged to the Abbey (see D. Howlett in *Manuscripts at Oxford, an Exhibition in Memory of R.W. Hunt*, Bodleian, 1980, p.85). The Bible lacked its first two leaves by 1964, so nothing remained of any St Albans ownership inscription, but since over 130 manuscripts survive from the great library of St Albans, and as there were no other abbeys in the town or neighbourhood, the Abbey flyleaves make it very probable that the Bible was once in the famous library there.

Fourteenth-century Bibles are surprisingly rare. Copies were made in such numbers between the late twelfth and the late thirteenth centuries that most monasteries were evidently well-supplied with copies for the rest of the Middle Ages. St Albans had two related monumental Bibles of the late twelfth century and two thirteenth-century copies, one at least acquired before the death of Matthew Paris in 1259, since it was annotated by him (see N.R. Ker, *Medieval Libraries*, 1964, pp.165-66). In the fourteenth century, however, St Albans was ruled by Michael of Mentmore, a notable scholar who is actually recorded in the Abbey chronicle as having provided his house with two fine Bibles, one for the monks' use and one for use in the abbot's study ('duas bonas Biblias, quarum unam dedit Conventus, alteram suo studio assignavit', *Gesta Abbatum*, Rolls Series, 1867, II, 363). Michael of Mentmore entered St Albans by 1326, became abbot in 1335 and died of the Black Death on 12 April 1349; the coincidence of date and the rarity of Bibles of the fourteenth century suggest that the book broken up in 1964 may very well correspond to one of the two Bibles mentioned in the chronicle. Michael of Mentmore is not known to have visited Paris but he did buy manuscripts from the estate of Richard de Bury, bishop of Durham and author of the *Philobiblion* (see A.B. Emden, *Biographical Register . . . Oxford*, 1958, II, 1260). As Richard de Bury was frequently in Paris in the 1320s and 30s and recorded that he bought and ordered many books there, it is just possible (though absolutely without proof) that the Bible was commissioned there by the best-known of all medieval English bibliophiles. At the very least, it has been in England since the Reformation and it almost certainly belonged to St Albans Abbey.

An Italian Book of Hours
circa 1375

MARGARET MANION

[State Library of South Australia, Adelaide]

In September of 1978 the Friends of the State Library of South Australia, Adelaide, purchased from Alan Thomas a small Book of Hours (102 by 79mm). It is written in a round gothic liturgical hand, and is embellished throughout with initials in burnished gold set against elaborate blue and red pen-flourished decoration. Each of the Hours of the two major offices and the other main sections of the book are introduced by a series of historiated initials devoted to the Passion of Christ (Office of the Passion and Cross); the Infancy of Christ and the Death and Assumption of the Virgin (the little Office of the Virgin); Christ in His Majesty (the Penitential Psalms) and the Virgin of Humility with a book (Votive Mass of the Virgin). These pages are also framed by a border of curling acanthus leaves variously intertwined with stems, knots, bars and interlace, and inhabited by drolleries, grotesques and energetic male nudes. A rich palette of blue, yellow, orange, green and pink is offset by the lavish use of burnished gold especially in the patterns of small schematic leaf-ends and rounded lobes, which are outlined in black and threaded through the border, and for the insets of the rectangular frames around the historiated initials.

Since its appearance in H.P. Kraus, Catalogue 80 (New York, 1956) this manuscript has been described in sales catalogues (Sotheby's, 13 July 1977, lot 39, and Alan Thomas, 1978) as a Book of Hours of Rome use, written and illuminated in Avignon between 1350 and 1375, probably for a member of the papal court resident there during the Babylonian Captivity. Probably because of some verses in the Calendar which were interpreted as referring to the papacy at Avignon, and a rubric attributing the Hours of the Cross to Pope John XXII, builder of the palace there, the works cited for comparison have been fourteenth-century volumes which found their way to Avignon but are mostly Neapolitan in style, reflecting that city's links with Anjou. These are the Missal of St Didier of Avignon (Avignon, MS 138), the Bible of Robert of Anjou (Vatican, MS Lat 14430), and a psalter auctioned at Sotheby's, 3 December 1968, lot 19, formerly Chester Beatty W.MS 71. The so-called

Missal of Clement VII (Avignon, MS 136), also cited for comparison, is Bolognese.

Careful examination of these manuscripts and related works, together with discussions with Mme Leonelli at the Musée du Petit Palais, Avignon, who is engaged in research on the Avignon School, and with M Avril of the Bibliothèque Nationale, Paris, have established that the Adelaide Hours has, in fact, nothing in common with this group apart from its fourteenth-century Italian origin. Moreover, the Calendar verses and the office rubric referred to above prove to have been in quite widespread use, and cannot be interpreted as evidence of Avignon provenance.

Of more significance, however, is the inclusion in the Calendar of a group of saints venerated in Tuscany and Umbria; namely St Mustiola of Chiusi (July 3), St Zerbonius of Elba (October 10), and St Herculanus of Perugia (March 1). For the decoration of the manuscript—the design of its border, its range of colour, and the style and iconography of its historiated initials—fits much more convincingly into the context of fourteenth-century central Italian illumination than into those of Neapolitan or Avignon circles. The distinctive features of local schools, with the interchange of influences through travelling artists, and the copying of compositions in Tuscan and Umbrian book illumination, have become the focus for more precise study only in recent times, and much detailed research is still required in this field. It is prudent, therefore, simply to state at this stage that the Adelaide Hours is central Italian, possibly Perugian, and was probably illuminated in about 1375.

Beyond laying the Avignon attribution to rest and locating the Adelaide Hours with reasonable confidence in a central Italian context, it is worth noting that the book is an interesting representative of a genre whose early development in Italy is still largely unplotted. Apart from northern examples, strongly influenced by French trends, fourteenth-century Italian Books of Hours are relatively rare in collections outside Italy and they do not feature prominently in studies and descriptive catalogues

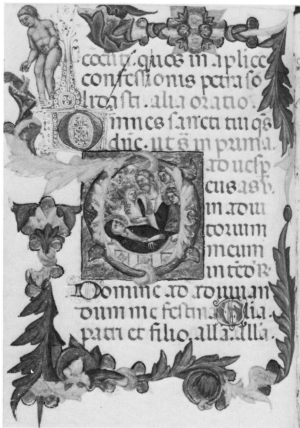

of Italian libraries. Certain distinctively Italian features are evident in the decorative programme of the Adelaide Hours. The Passion Cycle lays an emphasis on the Crucifixion and Burial of Christ. At Sext Christ is offered the sponge; at None blood issues from his pierced side and from his hands and feet; at Vespers the Virgin helps to place him in the tomb; at Compline she laments with attendants over his shrouded form. I am grateful to Dr Joanna Cannon for pointing out the similarity of this sequence to the one followed in the Pseudo-Bonaventura's *Meditations on the Life of Christ*, so popular at this time. In the Little Office of the Virgin both Vespers and Compline are devoted to the Death and Assumption of the Virgin, by contrast with French books where usually only Compline is illustrated by this theme. For the Penitential Psalms, a *Maiestas* image of Christ contrasts with the French pattern of a repentant David or a scene from his life. The Madonna of Humility introducing the votive Mass of the Virgin is, of course, of Sienese origin.

This small book reflects in its decorative layout and thematic programme the larger and more prevalent choir books and breviaries. However, it manages to achieve a spirit of reflective intimacy appropriate to its more personal function as a private prayer-book, no doubt for a person of rank and standing, given its sumptuous and detailed illumination.

Book of Hours, c. 1375. *Left: fol.93ʳ. Right: fol.96ᵛ.*
Foot: fol.15ʳ

14

Domenico Cavalca, *Vite dei Santi Padri*
Italy, early fifteenth century

KARL DACHS

Bayerische Staatsbibliothek, Munich

Munich has long enjoyed close cultural links with Italy and because of their geographic and intellectual proximity the Bayerische Staatsbibliothek is extraordinarily rich in Italian manuscripts and printed books. Travelling monks, students from the southern universities, and humanists, brought home large numbers of Latin manuscripts, and Italian princesses had valuable manuscripts in their dowries. The number of manuscripts in the Italian language is smaller, and yet even this diligently promoted category now numbers 906 manuscripts. About 200 of these have been purchased by the library in recent years with the conscientious help of Mr Alan G. Thomas, to whom we would like to show our appreciation and our thanks. Cod. ital. 691, one of the manuscripts acquired through him, is described here.

Its text is the Italian translation of the well-known Latin legendary, *Vitas Patrum*, the lives of the ancient hermits, which evolved from a Greek collection from early Christian settlements in the eastern Mediterranean. The Volgarizzamento—for a long time handed down anonymously—was initially attributed to the Dominican friar, Domenico Cavalca (1270-1342), in the edition published by G. Silvestri (Milan, 1830). Cavalca wrote other tracts and translations, all of a devotional nature, and he was called the 'padre della prosa italiana' by the literary critic Pietro Giordani (1774-1848). His principal work, the *Vite dei Santi Padri* is, strictly-speaking, a closely derivative text rather than a translation, as it far surpasses the quality of the Latin original and has always been admired by linguistic purists. It is actually difficult to withdraw from the magic of the fresh and animated prose which carries one over the frustration a modern reader may feel at the recurring accounts of the effortless ease with which the hermit heroes of the tale fight against 'melanconia', 'ebrietà', and the 'diletti carnali'.

In spite of linguists' fascination with the purity and balance of the text there is still no critical edition of this, the most perfect prose of the Trecento. Modern editions, including that of Sonio (1858) which claims to be critical, are ultimately only reprints of the harmonised text by Manni (Florence, 1731-32), using only a few manuscripts and several incunabula. Now, at least, two recent papers give information on the sources: Thomas Kaeppeli (*Scriptores Ordinis Praedicatorum Medii Aevi*, Rome, 1970, I 306 ff.) includes twenty-four manuscripts of which some are defective or only fragments. In addition there are two codices mentioned by Mr Thomas now in the Trivulziana, Milan (MS 544), and in the Bibliothèque Nationale, Paris (MS ital. 1712), together with this new manuscript in Munich. Only six of the manuscripts seem to be fourteenth-century, the rest being fifteenth-century. Most are on paper and only four are illuminated: the manuscripts at the Angelica in Rome, at the Trivulziana and the two in Paris and Munich. The rich tradition of this work in print is documented by Alfredo Cioni (*Bibliografia de 'Le Vite dei Santi Padri' volgarizzate da Fra Domenico Cavalca*, Florence, 1962, *Biblioteca degli eruditi e dei bibliofili*, 73), with excellent notes on the relationship between the different versions. In the incunabula period alone twenty editions were published between 1474 and 1499, and a further twenty-five editions were based on these before the attempt at a critical edition was published by Manni in 1731. If descriptions of the manuscripts and of the printed versions can be trusted, the various manuscripts differ so considerably from each other and from the early printed texts that it is likely that several different versions circulated at once.

A comparison of the Munich manuscript with Sonio's edition shows a difference in orthography in nearly every word and different expressions and sentence structure. Many insertions and deletions provide even more important differences. Some chapters even have only the theme in common. A specialist could perhaps localise the different copies by local peculiarities of language and spelling.

The present manuscript contains an almost complete text of parts I-IV (i.e., Sonio's edition, 1858, pp.13-312) lacking chapters 80, 86, 89, 93-95, 99, 101 and 135 in part III, and a whole quire in part IV, chapters 20-37 with the end of 19 and the beginning of 38. In part II an additional chapter is

Bayerische Staatsbibliothek, Cod. ital. 691, fol.106ʳ, 275x190mm

introduced between chapters 8 and 9. The manuscript is on vellum, 247 leaves, 275 by 190mm, Italian, from the first quarter of the fifteenth century. It is written in an early humanistic hand by three scribes (changes on fols 181ᵛ and 239ʳ). It has 264 illuminated initials (2 to 4 lines in height), 39 historiated initials with half-length figures of saints (2 to 5 lines in height), and all initials have penwork borders extending to half or the full height of the written area. At the beginning of each of the four books is a large historiated initial (*c.*70 by 70mm) showing (1) Saints Paul and Anthony sitting under a palm tree, (2 and 3) monks standing before an architectural background and (4) a saint distributing alms; each one has penwork borders surrounding the writing. The first page is very rubbed with the loss of a coat of arms. The manuscript

is bound in Italian eighteenth-century vellum, with no signs of provenance.

The early humanistic script of our manuscript provides some clues for the dating of the book. It belongs to the intermediate period (1375-1425) of the steady and conscious simplification of gothic script under the influence of Carolingian models, and some specific forms—such as the alternative **r**-forms with a clear preference for the archaic 2-shaped **r**, a constant change between **d** with a straight and with a curved ascender, and the absence of clubbed thickening of the ascenders of **b**, **d**, **h** and **l**—all place it in the first quarter of the fifteenth century. There can be no doubt that this manuscript will be very influential in any future research on Cavalca's *Vite dei Santi Padri*.

16

Administrative Documents for Normandy early fifteenth century

JEAN FURSTENBERG

Beaumesnil

I have known Alan Thomas for a great many years. Having lived in London twice in my long life, I received his catalogues and I read them with growing interest. They listed fine and rare items with descriptions which impressed me not only in terms of scholarship and erudition but also by their entertaining wit. Although there was no attempt at being comical, I discovered an amusing and wry sense of humour which is extremely rare in catalogues.

I decided that this man must be full of good sense and I went out to see his shop, more in order to make his acquaintance than with the hope of making any significant purchases. I remember finding Alan Thomas very pleasant and congenial, as I had expected.

Although I could not afford to purchase early illuminated manuscripts, and I did not collect early Bibles which were a specialty of his, I did acquire quite a few fine and rare books from Alan Thomas. Of special interest for me and for my foundation in Beaumesnil are some early-fifteenth-century manuscripts from the Phillipps collection which contain details of the appointments of governors in various areas of Normandy. These manuscripts, which consist of four large, untrimmed sheets of parchment, are in French, which was still the official language of England, and each appointment was issued by the Duke of York, Governor-General of Normandy in Rouen.

As it happens, one appointment concerns the flourishing town of Bernay, our market town, which was then the commercial centre for a number of important monasteries and their farms. The Castle of Beaumesnil, in fact, must have belonged to the territory of Bernay and was under English ownership: two generations of Willoughby, now called Willoughby de Broke. The new governor of Bernay, then serving the English but earlier owing allegiance to Burgundy and later to the King of Navarre, was instructed to live off the fat of the land; he was something of a condottiere. Another appointee, slightly further south, received more detailed instructions, as he was to levy an army around Vernon and was to be paid for it.

I fear that I am lapsing into local history, instead of communicating my friendly devotion to Alan Thomas, now reaching the age of a grown-up. I wish to convey not only my own greetings and congratulations but also those of the International Association of Bibliophiles, of which I am the Honorary Chairman. All the best, my dear Alan.

Honoré Bonet, *L'Arbre des batailles*
France, 1425

THOMAS H. REYNOLDS

Law Library, University of California, Berkeley

Robbins MS 91, a copy *L'Arbre des batailles*, was purchased from Alan G. Thomas nearly a year after I had first seen it in his home. He was familiar with the acquisition policies of the R.D. and S.M. Robbins Collection of the Law Library, and felt that the manuscript, being both rare and nearly contemporary, would appeal to us; the late Charles McCurry, the Law Library's research historian and canon law bibliographer, agreed, and the book reached Berkeley in April 1979.

I am indebted to Charles McCurry's successor Stephen Horwitz and to his colleague Stephanie Tibbets of the Institute of Medieval Canon Law for the codicological research on this manuscript. It is on paper, in excellent condition, and bound in faded red morocco attributed to Padeloup. It contains 127 numbered and three unnumbered folios, and the original first leaf has been removed and substituted by a seventeenth-century hand. The manuscript is otherwise complete in spite of a misnumbering in the foliation. The quiring is i-v^{12}, vi^{16}, vii-ix^{14}, x^{12}, with catchwords at the lower right of the versos. The paper now measures 274 by 210mm; from partial loss of some inconsequential marginalia we can deduce that the book has been trimmed at least once. In addition, the margins of many pages (almost certainly blank areas) have been cut away for scrap. There are three distinct watermarks, each comprising about a third of the manuscript: a bow and arrow (Briquet 809), a cluster of grapes (Briquet 13002) and a bull's head with lolling tongue (Briquet 14312). These suggest that the paper, at least, derived from Provence or Piedmont.

Pages are ruled in dry point and written in *littera cursiva textualis*, with between 29 and 34 long lines per side in bistre ink rubricated in red. The hand is sufficiently uniform to be regarded as the work of a single scribe. The colophon is dated 1425 and is signed 'Johannes de Quadrinno, clericus diocesis lemovicensis'. Limoges would be a not unlikely locale for the writing, although the watermarks suggest the possibility of a location further to the south-east. While not a sumptuously illuminated presentation copy, this is more than an ordinary working manuscript; it was most likely commissioned by a patron for his own use or as a gift.

The marginal notes are by two hands, apparently not later than the sixteenth century, one set by an early owner, probably monastic, who has signed the verso of the last blank 'Adhemarus'. Later the volume must have been part of a considerable library, since a note describes it as no.1150 in the 'bibliothèque de l'abbé de Terlan'. It also bears the book-plate of H.J.B. Clements who wrote on armorial bookstamps during the 1930s.

The *Arbre des batailles*, the first early modern work on the laws of war, was composed between 1386 and 1389, and dedicated to Charles VI. There is some confusion as to the correct spelling of Bonet's name. Although the form Honoré Bonet is recognised and accepted there is now reasonable evidence that the name was actually Bouvet (G. Ouy in *Romania*, 80, 1959, pp.255-59; N.A.R. Wright in *Recherches de théologie ancienne et médiévale*, 39, 1972, pp.116-19), and most censuses of manuscripts take the easy way out, using the Christian name Honoré. He was born in the early 1340s in Provence. By 1382, when he received his first degree in canon law at Avignon, he was a Benedictine monk of the monastery of Île-Barbe near Lyons. The degree of *doctor decretorum* was conferred in October 1386 at Avignon, by which time he was prior of Salon or Sellonet, a hamlet in the diocese of Ebrun; for the rest of his career he was anxious to exchange this insignificant benefice for a better one (see A. Coville, *La Vie intellectuelle dans les domaines d'Anjou – Provence de 1380 à 1435*, Paris, 1941, pp.214-318, and G.W. Coopland, *The Tree of Battles of Honoré Bonet*, Cambridge, Mass., 1949).

The *Arbre* is a primary source of considerable historical interest for the study of the origins of public international law and the history of church and state relations in the late Middle Ages. It is divided into four books of unequal length. The first deals with the general state of Christendom and the seemingly unresolvable situation of the Great Schism. Book II, on the fall of empires (Carthage, Rome, etc.) is substantially a re-working of ancient

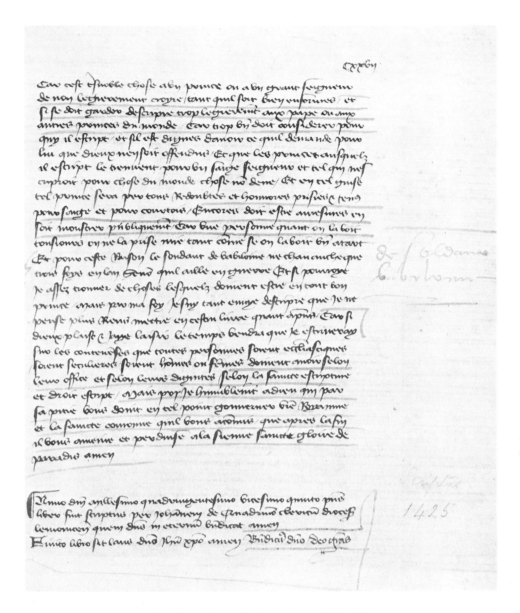

Fol.127ʳ, with scribal colophon, 274x210mm

history. Book III treats war in general and some aspects of strategy in particular, but it is Book IV (with some 132 chapters out of the work's total of 171) which represents the *Arbre's* claim to be regarded as a source. It touches on all aspects of warfare: on the treatment of prisoners and non-combatants, spoils and ransoms, the duties of soldiers and officers, self-defence and fealty, truces and ambassadors, and champions. Bonet was surprisingly compassionate and free of prejudice in his chapters on Jews and Saracens, although his assertion of the just war, however carefully hedged by conditions, proves troublesome to a modern reader. In this section, Bonet took the Church's recognised laws for the regulation of private wars and applied them to public wars. In the twilight of the feudal age, a period of organised anarchy and regulated violence, the chivalric pleasures and profits of private warfare were limited to noblemen,

but the results were endured by all. Bonet was greatly influenced by his own experiences (in 1392 he was driven from his monastery by the brutal Raymond of Turenne, one of the most rapacious freebooters of the period). Bonet's book was an attempt to regularise warfare, emphasising the requirements of discipline and loyalty (not common traits in feudal times) and even providing a guide to battle itself, as well as a political tract in support of the French monarchy.

Even before 1387, Bonet had become involved in the affairs of the House of Anjou. He sent illuminated copies of the *Arbre* to Charles VI and the Dukes of Berry and Burgundy and he was awarded a royal pension in 1389. His last years were spent in Paris in the Dominican house of Jean de Meun. He probably died in about 1409. It is safe to venture that the Robbins manuscript of the *Arbre* is one of the earliest dated copies of the book.

Customary of the Shrine of St Thomas Becket Canterbury, 1428

D.H.TURNER

British Library

Some people know what started them off. I cannot recall any one event which turned my thoughts towards the history of art and liturgy and music, principally as revealed on the pages of manuscripts. I do know that an important step was buying a Roman Missal from Alan Thomas when I was in my late teens. The book is on my desk as I write. It is a product of the house of Pustet at Regensburg in 1909: *Missale Romanum ex decreto sacrosancti Concilii Tridentini restitutum . . . Ratisbonae, Romae, Neo Eboraci & Cincinnati. Sumptibus et typis Friderici Pustet . . . .*

Towards the end of the 1940s I paid a visit to Bournemouth where I discovered Alan Thomas's bookshop. It was just what I thought, and still think, a bookshop should be: several rooms filled with books on shelves from floor to ceiling, and stacked on tables. One was welcome to browse indefinitely. This I did, and the understanding proprietor let me stay on after the shop closed, as he was remaining himself. Eventually I made two purchases, the *Missale Romanum* and a nineteenth-century *Book of Common Prayer*. The second I no longer have, but the Missal was the first true liturgical book I owned and it has served me well as a primer for liturgical studies and a manual of devotion.

After I joined the Department of Manuscripts of the British Museum in 1956 the name of Alan G. Thomas soon became known to me as that of a bookseller of distinction, and I identified him as the understanding proprietor of the bookshop in Bournemouth. We met again and I am proud of an acquaintance which has continued to the present day when Alan, having removed to London, has become an elemental spirit of the bibliographical world. My department has been fortunate in acquiring a number of interesting manuscripts from him, of which the best is undoubtedly the Customary of the Shrine of St Thomas Becket. This was written in 1428 by two monks of Christ Church, Canterbury, John Vyel and Edmund Kyngyston, who then held the office of guardians of the shrine. They prefixed it to a late-thirteenth-century manuscript in their possession, containing Benedict of St Alban's life of Becket, compiled between 1183 and 1189, and Guernes de Pont-Sainte-Maxence's account of the saint, which was composed between 1172 and 1174. The whole volume came into the hands of the mighty Sir Thomas Phillipps and Alan Thomas bought it for stock at the tenth of the new series of Phillipps sales, on 26 November 1975. The British Library purchased the manuscript from him on December 18th that same year, with the help of generous contributions from the Friends of the National Libraries and Dr W.G. Urry.

The Customary and the Lives of Becket have been catalogued as Additional MS 59616. The manuscript measures 350 by 250mm, and it comprises vii + 142 folios. Eleven folios of information about one of the richest and most famous shrines in Christendom, the chief place of pilgrimage in England, make up the Customary. Dan John and Dan Edmund carefully rehearse such things as liturgical observances, security precautions, arrangements for visitors, and payments from the revenues. Being a contemporary and official record theirs is a more valuable source than recollections, possibly not by a monk, like those in the *Rites of Durham*. In the *Canterbury Cathedral Chronicle*, no.70, pp.19-20, I excerpted details about the feast of the Translation of St Thomas Becket, on July 7th. I will mention here the provisions for pilgrims to the feast of his Passion on December 29th. On the eve the guardians received from the cellarer seven monastic loaves, seven pounds of cheese, and seven gallons of beer, and—from the kitchen—sufficient coals. They gave the bearer of the coals 1d. and the bearer of the other things 2d. During the night, at a suitable time, when the bells were ringing for matins, the guardians opened the gates of the shrine precinct to the waiting people. Many of these had come full of excitement at the prospect of hearing the reading, customary on that occasion, of Becket's life 'clearly in the mother tongue'. The life read was that by Guernes de Pont-Sainte-Maxence, in French, and the book from which it was read was that of which we treat. Afterwards the two secular clerks who served the guardians invited

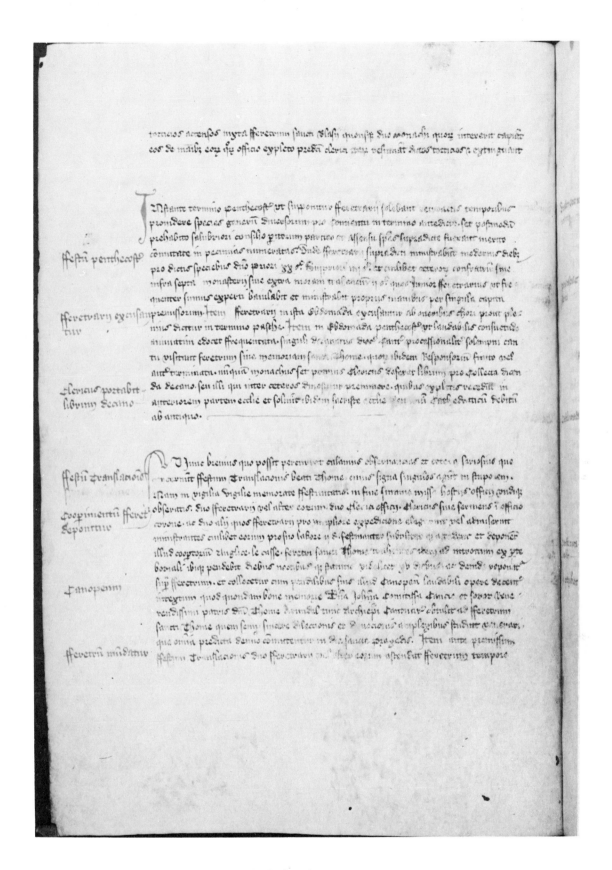

Fol.8ᵛ, 350x250mm

the people, who were perhaps fatigued, to warm themselves at a fire that had been made ready and to refresh themselves with bread and cheese, and beer. Of all glimpses of the Middle Ages that I know I find this one of the most vivid: the pilgrims eating by the fire in the early morning in Canterbury Cathedral in mid-winter.

21

Durandus, *Rationale Divinorum Officiorum* Mainz, 1459

JERRY D.CAMPBELL

Bridwell Library, Southern Methodist University, Dallas

. . . the first work, from the pen of an uninspired writer, ever printed—Neale and Webb (1842)

This phrase was once the description of William Durandus' most popular work. And yet, were the meanings of phrases as durable as the book described, we would see in that statement more than slight praise. The *Rationale* first appeared in print on 6 October 1459, from the press of Fust and Schoeffer in Mainz. It had been preceded in print by four works—the Bible, a Missal, a Psalter, and a Latin grammar by Donatus. The Donatus grammar survived only in fragments, thus leaving the work of Durandus as the oldest complete non-biblical printed book.

This work was the bargain brought back to his bookshop by Alan G. Thomas, Bookseller. The world is full of retail merchants, but those who trade in books are like no others. The objects of their livelihood are no mere commodities. They are fascinated by this printed substance of human thought and art and are driven to own it, if only temporarily, as it patiently makes its way through the more transient medium of human hands. The *Rationale* was a book to own for many reasons.

It was in its creation an exemplar, introducing into print that type style some have called gotico-antiqua or fere-humanistica. The tall gothic type of the 42-line Bible and the Mainz Psalter would not suit the simple needs of less formal, scholarly works of which this would be only the first of many. The printers, therefore, specified the type style, a minuscule, that had become the standard book-hand of Latin Europe. It was the style that with the advent of printing in Italy evolved into the Roman type. And it would be the style reflected in the nineteenth-century rebirth of fine printing in William Morris's Troy and Chaucer types.

The *Rationale* was, as well, a work with important content. It was in its day by far the most thorough and detailed, though somewhat fanciful, explanation of 'The Significance of the Divine Offices' to have been written. It constituted the modern equivalent of a textbook in medieval liturgics that soared to great popularity through at least forty-four editions before 1501 (*GKW*). It remains for the modern scholar of liturgics an indispensable source for the reconstruction of medieval worship.

With both exemplary type style and sought-after text, the 1459 *Rationale* was the epitome of the printed scholarly book. All copies were printed on durable and fine vellum to withstand the touch of many searching hands. The pages were clean and simple with ample margins to please the eye and ease the burden of reading. The work was not illustrated in the first edition. However, the potential monotony from a book with words only was avoided by the use of decorated initials printed from metal blocks. These were graceful, almost lyrical, in design, yet possessing the dignity and discipline befitting the character of a work on the liturgy. 'This idea,' as Mr Thomas averred, 'was brilliant, the result breathtaking, but the process was too time-consuming and expensive to be practical. In the Durandus there are two 13-line and three 7-line examples of this famous process, but it was never used again' (Catalogue 39). The book as object, therefore, expertly served the reason for its existence. It aesthetically engaged the reader, eased the rigour of scholarly reading, and complemented the subject of the text in its artistic character.

As might be the fate of a survivor of 522 years, this copy of the *Rationale* is somewhat battered, though no less majestic as a result. On eighty-four leaves the broad lower margins have been cut away. The reason for such trimming will most likely remain a subject for speculation, but the bibliophile may be permitted the hope that ignorance rather than malice was the perpetrator. The tall stately folio also bears evidence of care and respect: an ancient patch with text restored here and a mended tear there. The reader may be assured that among those who owned the book were some who understood its importance.

Alan G. Thomas was such a person. His choice of the 1459 *Rationale* as the single book to carry to a colleague who was nearing the end of his life belied his own feigned ignorance of the significance of the book (*The Book Collector*, 28, Winter, 1979, p.552).

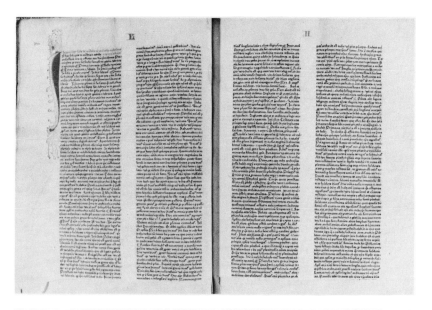

hijs q̃ ſut foris . Per iacinctũ·q̃ ē coloris aerei ſig̃-
ficat ſereitas ɔſcie·quã intra ſe potiſex oꝫ habe·ſcɔꝫ
qɔ oicit apl's·Ol'a nꝛahec ē teſhomũ ɔſcietie nꝛe.

Liber q̃rtus de miſſa τ ſingulis que in miſſa agunt·

Nter cuncta ecclefie ſacramenta
illud conſtat eſſe precipuuꝫ qɔ in
miſſe officio ſupra meſaꝫ ſacratiſſi-
mi celebrat altaris·illud ecclehe
repreſentans conuiuium in quo
filio reuertenti pater occidit vitu-
lum ſagmatum panem vite et
vinum quod miſcuit ſapientia proponent·hoc
autem officium criſtus inſtituit cum nouum condi-
dit teſtamentum·diſponens heredibus ſuis regnũ
ſicut pater ſuus ſibi diſpoſuit·vt ſuper menſam eius

Top: opening. Centre: detail. Bottom: binding covers

Book of Hours attributed to Jean Fouquet
France, *circa* 1465-75

CHARLOTTE LACAZE

[Comites Latentes Collection, Geneva]

The subject of this piece is a Book of Hours, Comites Latentes, MS 38, in which the figurative decoration now consists only of sixteen superb historiated initials. Without these, the manuscript would be difficult to localise, since its Calendar is missing and the Suffrages yield no significant information. The style of *camaïeu d'or* on coloured ground, however, links the book to the name of Jean Fouquet. This has always been recognised.

While the manuscript was in the Chester Beatty Collection (W.MS 83), Eric Millar recorded the opinions of Sir Sydney Cockerell, who believed 'them—*the initials*—to be by Fouquet', and Klaus Perls, who 'considers the 2 last, fols 72, 77, to be by Fouquet'. Sotheby's catalogue of the 1969 Chester Beatty sale suggested 'that the whole series is by a single artist, who was more probably a follower of Fouquet than the master himself'. 'Faced by this divergence of opinion among my peers', Alan Thomas remarked in his catalogue (23, 4) shortly afterwards, 'I can only recall the undergraduate who, when asked to name the Minor Prophets, answered "Who am I, that I should distinguish between Holy Men?"; I will content myself by stating that these miniatures contain the most exquisite work which has ever passed through my hands.' Since then, Claude Schaefer has classified the manuscript among Fouquet workshop products (*Recherches sur l'iconologie et la stylistique de l'art de Jean Fouquet*, Lille, 1971, II, 268), and Nicole Reynaud's recent catalogue for the commendable Fouquet exhibition follows this judgement (*Jean Fouquet. Les dossiers du département des peintures*, 22, Paris, Musée du Louvre, 1981, no.6J).

A rigorous stylistic analysis of the initials reveals two hands, with differences in execution and, more important, in compositional concepts. The first group comprises those initials without spatial setting with figures placed on the surface of the picture plane (fols 13, 21, 40, 53 and 66) or defining space by their own positions or moving in a spatial setting created by objects placed at angles to the picture plane (fols 1, 7, 17, 19, 24, 49 and 55). In contrast to this group of initials, the remaining four contain compositions which transmit a remarkable sensation of three-dimensionality: the Shepherds, David, the Fifth and Sixth Days of Creation (fols 15, 26, 72 and 77). All four scenes are composed of figures placed obliquely behind the pictorial surface and in front of distant atmospheric landscapes. This kind of composition presupposes a concept of the image as a self-contained entity behind the framing letter which acts as a window on an imaginary world beyond the page of the book. The extraordinary evocation of depth is combined with a firm modelling of three-dimensional volume in a most delicate pointillistic application of the *camaïeu d'or* painting technique. This work betrays the skill of a painter even superior to the fine artist of the first group of initials. We suggest that this superior painter was Jean Fouquet himself.

The technique of painting in *camaïeu d'or*, probably first used by Fouquet in the enamels around the Melun Diptych (Reynaud no.6), occurs

[continued from page 22]

It was, Mr Thomas knew, a book of such merit that it would provide his friend a last occasion for joy over a bibliographical treasure. And others have owned and cared for this book, though most remain anonymous. The English red morocco Harleian binding executed by Christopher Chapman points us towards Robert Harley (1661-1724), first Earl of Oxford. Passing through his estate into the hands of the bookseller Thomas Osborne, the book again disappeared to emerge much later in the library of the New York financier, Carl Pforzheimer. It passed from the Pforzheimer library into the hands of Alan Thomas.

The provenance is brought up-to-date with Bridwell Library, Southern Methodist University. For many good and sufficient reasons Bridwell Library, with the help of Alan G. Thomas, Bookseller, has become the most recent owner of 'the first work from the pen of an uninspired writer ever printed'.

Top: detail from fol.15ʳ.
Bottom: fol.77ʳ, 165x105mm

in all the manuscripts by or attributed to him and his atelier. Yet Fouquet's own handling of the technique differed from that of his followers. He built up his volumes with tiny touches of the brush which are allowed to form solid patches only where direct light hits the figures; the painter of the first group used long parallel strokes following the fall of the drapery and forming larger planes of solid gold colour. The differences are subtle, but they are noticeable and revealing.

The four initials here attributed to Fouquet display all the characteristics of his personal style: very light pointillism, volumetric figures placed at angles to the picture surface, fine aerial perspective and stable compositions where man and nature form one (see Otto Pächt in *Journal of the Warburg and Courtauld Institutes*, 4, 1941, and in *Jahrbuch der Kunsthistorischen Sammlungen in Wien*, 70, 1974, as well as Focillon and König, cited by Reynaud). Furthermore, very precise comparisons can be drawn between these four initials and known works of Fouquet. For example, the Creator on fol.77 is identical with the figure of Christ in the Hours of Etienne Chevalier (facsimile edited by Sterling and Schaefer, 1971, pl.13), Eve in the same initial is a twin to the wild women beneath the scene of the Conversion of St Paul (Sterling/Schaefer, pl.32),

25

Martial, *Epigrammata*
Naples, *circa* 1480

BRIAN S. CRON

Kew

When the Abbey-Hornby manuscripts were sold at Sotheby's in 1974 and 1975, I little thought that two from that splendid array would one day enhance my small collection. That they now do, was brought about in the following way.

In the early summer of 1977 I called on Alan Thomas intending to look at some of his printed books and certainly with no money available for buying manuscripts. A small book in a slip-case caught my eye. On removing it from its case I decided at once that, somehow, I must have it. The book was a copy of Martial's *Epigrams* written at Naples, one of three Martial manuscripts in the Hornby collection. It was priced far higher than I could afford at that time. To my disappointment Alan told me that he would have been only too happy to negotiate had he not already offered it, together with another manuscript, to a famous German library from whom he expected a decision within about ten days. I then waited with some impatience, and on learning that Alan had not heard from Germany, I called on him again. He had another Hornby manuscript available, a splendid fifteenth-century Caesar, probably from Ferrara, and although it was twice as expensive as the Martial I decided to look upon it as my second choice in the event of losing the battle for the little Neapolitan charmer. I returned home and occupied my time by considering what early printed books I would have to offer in exchange for the Martial; in order to make certain of the deal I turned out the majority of the fifteenth- and sixteenth-century books that I had collected over the previous eight or nine years. It was, I think, over three weeks before I heard the good news that the Martial was available and that the German library had chosen the other manuscript offered. Alan very kindly brought both the Martial and the Caesar to my home with the result that he took away the printed books and I kept the two manuscripts. The success of this transaction was entirely a consequence of Alan's understanding of my circumstances, and I am confident that the pleasure of the deal was equally divided between us.

As the Martial has been fully described by J.J. G Alexander and A.C. de la Mare (*The Italian Manuscripts in the Library of Major J.R. Abbey*, London, 1969, pp.84-85) I will provide only a summary description here. The manuscript is in a near italic script and was executed in Naples about

---

[continued from page 24]

the pointillistic trees and the evocation of dense forest resemble the same subject in the *camaïeu d'or* bas-relief beneath the Birth of St John the Baptist (Sterling/Schaefer, pl.29), and the examples could easily be multiplied.

By now one may wonder why such an important and busy painter as Jean Fouquet would have contributed only four historiated initials to a Book of Hours where even the most important subjects at the beginning of the codex were left to an assistant. The answer is simply that the master did not only paint these four initials. The manuscript is missing not only the Calendar but a number of full-page miniatures (the liturgical analysis of the manuscript is due to R.P. Robert Amiet) and *lacunae* exist after fols 25 and 54 and most likely after fols 71, 76, and elsewhere. Given Fouquet's talent for inventing new iconography, one cannot even guess at the subjects of these miniatures. Perhaps they still exist, detached, among 'the most exquisite work' in their respective collections.

The Comites Latentes manuscript measures 165 by 105mm with a justification of 122 by 78mm. It was last rebound, and probably slightly cropped, by Duquesne in Ghent in the late nineteenth century. Its style suggests it was executed between 1465 and 1475, close in date to the single page by Jean Fouquet in the Hours of Charles of France (Reynaud no.19). This miniature, a night scene painted in *camaïeu d'or*, could serve as a guide in the search for the lost miniatures of the Comites Latentes manuscript, treasures which, if rediscovered, would add to the sparse survivals of Jean Fouquet's oeuvre.

26

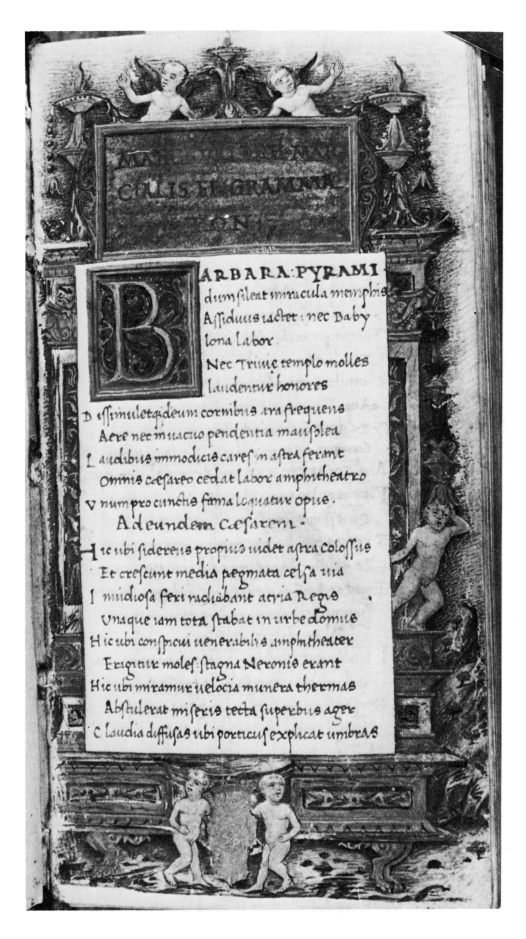

BARBARA PYRAMI
dum sileat miracula memphis
Assiduus iactet : nec Baby
lona labor.
Nec Triuie templo molles
laudentur honores
Dissimuletq; deum cornibus ara frequens
Aere nec in uacuo pendentia mausolea
Laudibus immodicis cares in astra ferunt
Omnis cæsareo cedat labor amphitheatro
Vnum pro cunctis fama loquatur opus.
Ad eundem cæsarem.
Hic ubi sidereus propius uidet astra colossus
Et crescunt media pegmata celsa uia
Inuidiosa feri radiabant atria Regis
Vnaque iam tota stabat in urbe domus
Hic ubi conspicui uenerabilis amphitheater
Erigitur moles: stagna Neronis erant
Hic ubi miramur uelocia munera thermas
Abstulerat miseris tecta superbus ager
Claudia diffusas ubi porticus explicat umbras

Book 1, fol.1ʳ, 144x77mm

The Will of Jankyn Smyth Bury St Edmunds, 1481

TOSHIYUKI TAKAMIYA

Tokyo

I find it more than gratifying to be able to celebrate Alan Thomas's seventieth birthday as well as the 500th anniversary of the Guildhall Feoffment Trust of Bury St Edmunds combined charities, founded in 1481 by Jankyn Smyth, by presenting below the former's admirable account of the latter's will, with some corrections and additions which I have incorporated into it.

The Will of Jankyn Smyth (d.1481) with details of his benefactions and a rental of the lands which he bequeathed to the town of Bury St Edmunds, with the will of Margaret Odiham (d.1492) and a rental of the lands which she too bequeathed to the town, in Middle English, with a few portions in Latin, manuscript on vellum, 33 leaves (last 4 blank) plus original flyleaf, text complete, lacks a blank after fol.7, with stub remaining, quires mostly of 8 leaves (ii⁴, iii⁶) with one catchword on fol.17ᵛ, signatures partly visible on fols 9, 12 and 14, pagination in quire i by a later hand, modern foliation throughout in pencil, ruling in brown ink, pricking holes intact on fols 8-17 (quires ii and iii), single columns mostly of 32 lines, but in quire i lines varying from 26 to 41, the colour of ink varying from dark to light brown, written by no less than seven scribes mostly in a regular gothic bookhand fere-anglicana, some headings in textura script, rubrics on fols 8 and 20, some paragraph

---

[continued from page 26]

1480-90. It has 204 leaves and measures 144 by 77mm. The first page was illuminated by Cristoforo Majorana and there are white vine-stem-type initials to each of the remaining books. The first letter and the title of every epigram, and the first line and title of every book, are in gold. The binding of purple velvet over wooden boards may be original and the erased coat of arms at the foot of the first page is probably that of Alfonso, Duke of Calabria. In the Abbey catalogue Dr de la Mare pointed out the resemblance of the script to that of a certain Clemens Salernitanus, and she has now told me that she is quite certain that he was the scribe of my manuscript. She also tells me of two further small manuscripts, in addition to those mentioned in the catalogue, that are signed by that scribe. They are a Florus in the Vatican (MS Barb. lat. 7) and a Tibullus with Vergil's Bucolics and Georgics in Wolfenbüttel (Herzog August Bibliothek Cod. 63.5. Aug. 8°). In addition to the similarity of script, both of the other small manuscripts are approximately the same size as mine and both have decoration attributed to Majorana at the beginning. A magnificent copy of Tacitus in Vienna (National Library, MS 49) was almost certainly illuminated by Majorana and the colour reproduction in F. Unterkircher's *European Illuminated Manuscripts in the Austrian National Library* (London, 1967),

pl.35, gives a good idea of his work.

This is not the occasion to expatiate on the pleasures of Martial's *Epigrams*. He caters for all tastes. The details he gives of ancient books are known to all who concern themselves with such things. The day-to-day life of Rome under both Domitian and the early Antonines is depicted with wit and skill in his small poems. He wrote more than fifteen hundred epigrams and each one in my manuscript is adorned with a title and initial letter in gold as mentioned above. This produces a pleasing effect, particularly in Books XIII and XIV which consist more or less entirely of two-line epigrams. As the poet himself says, at the beginning of Book XIV, 'versibus explicitum est omne duobus opus—lemmata si quaeris cur sint adscripta, docebo, ut, si malueris, lemmata sola legas'. ('The entire work is set out in couplets. If you ask why there are titles, I will tell you—so that, if you prefer, you may read the titles alone'). I hope Alfonso of Calabria, if he was the owner, appreciated the artistry of this little book.

I am not qualified to judge the merit of the text. A late manuscript such as this may even have been copied from one of the fifteenth-century printed editions. However that may be, I consider myself to be fortunate in owning a book which provides such interest and satisfaction in so many respects.

marks in red, a ten-line large initial in blue with full-length red penwork on fol.8, many later annotations and sidenotes, a few stains and some rubbing, minimal worming on the first leaves, contemporary binding, 224 by 145mm, secundo folio: Yaxle home. Bury St Edmunds, late 15th century. Present location: Toshiyuki Takamiya Collection, Tokyo. Provenance: this is apparently the original volume which belonged to the Candlemas Guild of Bury St Edmunds which every year on 2 February was 'red beforn the said bretheryn of that Gylde (fol.10) recording the benefactions made to them by Jankyn Smyth and Margaret Odiham. On the final pastedown are lists of names both of the 'vewers of Jankyn Smyths land' and the 'vewers of Marg. Odham land'. On the front

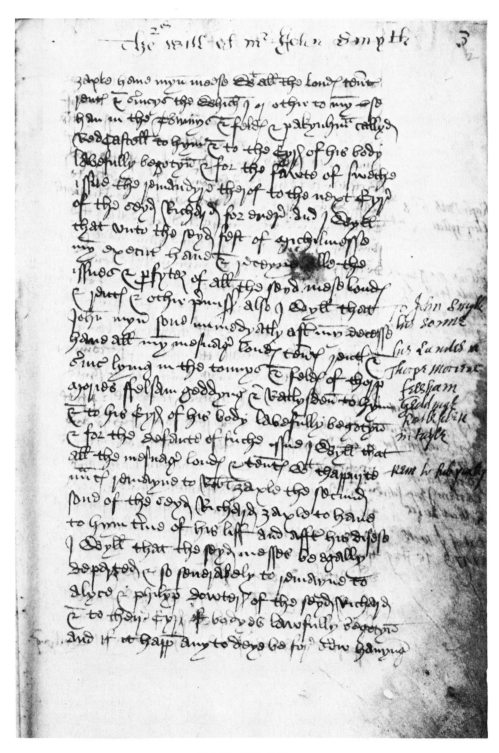

Fol.2ʳ, 224x145mm

29

pastedown is the name of 'Robard turner de eivsdem anno domini M. qun. & xxv' (1525). The volume was evidently still in Bury in 1650 when the will of Jankyn Smyth was confirmed (fol.9ᵛ).

Text: on the floor of St Mary's Church, Bury St Edmunds, is the brass of John or Jankyn Smyth (the two names are used without distinction, both in the literature on brasses and in the present manuscript) and his wife, kneeling with raised hands. Jankyn Smyth was a major benefactor of the church and of the town. He built the chancel aisles of the church (according to Pevsner) and is reputed to have given the Guildhall to the town. He is said too to have endowed the sermon which is preached every Thursday after Plough Monday, the oldest endowed sermon in England. For the brass, see E. Farrer, *A List of the Monumental Brasses . . . in the County of Suffolk* (1903), p.13; H.W. Macklin, *The Brasses of England*, (1928), p.200; A. Mee, *Suffolk* (1941), p.88; N. Pevsner, *Suffolk* (1961), p.128.

The present contemporary and official record of Smyth's benefactions opens with the full text of his will (fol.1) which includes the provision—very important for the identification of the brass—that his body was 'to be buryed in the Chirche of *our* lady in the towne of Bury befor seyd, in the North ele, befor the dor of the awhgter of Seynt John' (fol.1).

The will gives a detailed and fascinating list of bequests to numerous named institutions and individuals. He gives 'myn best stondying cuppe of siluer & gylt' to the Prior of Bury St Edmunds Abbey and to his successors, and financial gifts to the sacristan, priests and monks of the Abbey. He gives money to many religious houses including the Franciscans of Badwell (founded in 1263), the Dominicans of Sudbury (founded before 1247), the Augustinians of Clare (probably founded in 1248), both houses of friars in Thetford (there were both Augustinian and Dominican houses there), the nuns of Some in Cambridgeshire, the Benedictine nuns of Ickleton, and to the Augustinian nuns of Campsey. He evidently had close connections with the Franciscan nunnery of Bruisyard since he gave them 66s. 8d. to pray for his soul and 10 marks to dame Margaret Yaxle, sister of the house, and other gifts to other members of the Yaxle family. Of interest is the sum of 40s. given to the Augustinian convent of Ixworth 'to the reparacion of the same place', a gift apparently insufficient for the purpose since in 1514 Bishop Nykke found the convent buildings partly ruined and the windows poorly glazed, a roof leaking, and the abbey clock broken

(*VCH, Suffolk*, II, 105-106). Smyth gives furthermore, besides considerable expenses (carefully detailed) for his own funeral (and no doubt this would include the cost of the brass), money to his servants (named) and others, and all his lands in Bury to the 'ynhabytauntys' of Bury St Edmunds (as 'pleynly aperith' elsewhere in the present volume), and the manor of Brettys at Hepworth to establish a chantry and for the chaplain of the Guild of Jesus to sing for his soul.

His will is dated 12 December 1480. It is followed by the grant of probate of the will before John Swaffham, sacristan of Bury, dated 20 September 1481. Jankyn Smyth's will has been printed by S. Tymms, *Wills and Inventories from the Registers of the Commissary of Bury St Edmund's and the Archdeacon of Sudbury*, Camden Society 49 (1850), pp.55-61; Margaret Odiham's will has itself been calendared by V.B. Redstone, 'Calendar of Pre-Reformation Wills. Testaments . . . registered at the Probate Office of Bury St Edmunds', in *Proceedings of Suffolk Institute of Archaeology and Natural History*, 12 (1907), no.9, p.160. Binding: contemporary binding of tawed white leather over bevelled wooden boards sewn onto four leather thongs, stub remains on upper cover of red-stained strap (broken away), tall brass pin with quatrefoil mount on lower cover, binding slightly worn.

This is a fine example of a late medieval binding with the bands threaded through the outside of the boards and pegged in two triangular patterns (see G. Pollard, 'Describing Medieval Bookbindings' in *Medieval Learning and Literature: Essays presented to Richard William Hunt*, edited by J.J.G. Alexander and M.T. Gibson, Oxford, 1976, especially pp.56-57 ascribing the style to 1350-1459). It is an exceptionally late example of a tawed leather binding, very rarely found after 1450 (see Graham Pollard 'The Names of Some English 15th-Century Binders', *The Library*, 5th series, 25 (1970), especially pp 197-98). Perhaps by the late fifteenth century Bury was no longer in the forefront of artistic development, and the present binding is very conservative.

Postscript
While this volume was in the press I learnt from William R. Serjeant, County Archivist of Suffolk County Council, that they possess a manuscript of the will of John Smyth which is in many ways similar to the one mentioned above. Their manuscript bears the pressmark H1/2/1.

The Book of St Albans
1486

LOTTE HELLINGA

British Library

On the 5th June 1961, Sotheby's offered as lot 37 in their catalogue of Manuscripts, Printed Books and Americana of the late Apsley Cherry-Garrard a copy of The Book of St Albans, 1486, by the mysterious Schoolmaster Printer. The copy contained only 52 out of 90 leaves and signs of heavy use. Sotheby's mentioned these imperfections and added discouragement by noting damp stains, some paper repairs, and a modern binding by Zaehnsdorf. Yet the copy could not fail to attract attention, for all that.

> Perhaps no early English book has provided greater fascination among English speaking book-collectors over the last two hundred years than The Book of St Albans. The provenance of the few remaining copies reads like a trumpet call of famous collectors: Roxburghe, Spencer, Ashburnham, Carysfort, Pembroke, Brooke, Fitzwilliam, Aldenham, Hoe, Dyson Perrins, Bute, Huntington, Pierpont Morgan. But all this refers to about seventeen surviving copies, most of them imperfect, which have been fiercely fought for in auction battles, and at least eleven of which have now come to rest in permanent public collections.

Thus Alan G. Thomas, the successful bidder, in his Catalogue 9 of 1961. In spite of its imperfections this copy had graced the collections of Bromley-Davenport, Dyson Perrins and Walter Hutchinson before going to Cherry-Garrard. Whatever its state of preservation, Mr Thomas went on, the Book of St Albans remains an English collector's item par excellence: 'THE FIRST ENGLISH SPORTING BOOK, THE FIRST ENGLISH PRINTED ARMORIAL, THE FIRST ENGLISH BOOK WITH POPULAR RHYMES', and it contains 'THE FIRST COLOUR PRINTING IN ENGLAND'.

But Mr Thomas had discovered something that gave to this copy, however imperfect, a special significance for the history of English printing. He noticed that some of the manuscript markings appeared in a sort of pattern, corresponding with the page-endings of the second edition of the work, printed in Westminster ten years later by Wynkyn de Worde. The many marginal scribbles were in fact written by a press-editor in the process of preparing the St Albans book for the new edition. They reveal what in the St Albans text was acceptable to a Westminster printer in 1496, and, more important, what was not. It is an example of the rapid transformation of both visual and linguistic form and style at the end of the fifteenth century, an example that can hardly be surpassed in immediacy.

Only a small number of manuscripts which served as printer's copy in the fifteenth century are known. So far about sixteen have been recorded and seven of those document printing in England. Printer's copy is the most direct way we have of illuminating printing-house practice, its effect on textual transmission, and the transition from manuscript to print in general. The example of printer's copy discovered by Alan G. Thomas, however, is the first—and so far the only—known copy of a printed book used as printer's copy in the fifteenth century. To be able to observe the transition from copy to print within one medium has a value all of its own. There was, therefore, every justification for printing in the catalogue in bold black type: **THE BLACK TULIP OF ENGLISH INCUNABULA**.

Before the book was offered in the catalogue (at £12,500), Mr Thomas had consulted George D. Painter, then Assistant Keeper responsible for incunabula at the British Museum. Painter fully confirmed the conclusions that Mr Thomas had reached, and would have failed in his duties had he not remarked that a book of this significance should find a place in the national collection, although he was aware that these discoveries gave it a market value that the nation could not afford.

By the time the catalogue appeared Mr Thomas must have made up his mind; the book was to go to the British Museum. And although he had an immediate offer for it he let the Museum have it at about a quarter of the catalogue price. It was an act of sheer unselfish generosity that has so far remained unrecorded, for the national collection can at times be strangely reticent about its benefactors when sums of money do in fact change hands.

The purchase was recorded by Painter in *The*

British Museum Quarterly, 27 (1963-4), 100-101, as a noteworthy acquisition of the Department of Printed Books, and the book is on permanent exhibition in the King's Library. A comprehensive description of The Book of St Albans has now been completed for the *Catalogue of Books printed in the XVth Century now in the British Museum (BMC)*, of which volume XI, *England*, edited by the present author and Paul Needham, is now is preparation.

The significance of the St Albans copy is explained in the section describing Wynkyn de Worde's edition of 1496, for it is the process of producing the later edition that is revealed by the St Albans book. Press-editing in de Worde's printing house, casting off, and marking by the compositor, represent successive stages of the production of the book. In combination they bring us close to the hands that made the book, to the many small decisions which add up to the result we know, the book as issued by its printer.

Painter and the present author prepared this section successively. Here follows a preview of this small portion of *BMC* XI, dedicated to Alan G. Thomas as tribute to his happy discovery and generous spirit:

A copy of the edition printed at St Alban's (1486), Duff 56, was used as printer's copy for the present edition. Part of this copy is still extant. It is IB.55712, catalogued below. Its use in the printer's shop is shown by manuscript annotations and marks which reveal some of the practices of Wynkyn de Worde's press-editor and compositors. IB.55712 consists of quires e-f, ²a-e, comprising the 'Books of Hunting and of Coat Armour', and all but the last quire of 'Blasing of Arms', corresponding to c6ᵃ-g3ᵃ, ²a1ᵃ-²d1ᵃ of Wynkyn de Worde's edition. IB.55712 is hereafter referred to as **SA**, Wynkyn de Worde's edition as **W**.

Three phases can be distinguished in the marks and annotations in **SA**, the first of which is press-editing, revealed by editorial annotation. A number of corrections were made in one hand. These are sparing in the 'Book of Hunting', and are all followed by **W** apart from one erroneous alteration on f3ᵃ,l.6. The red-printed words displaced by faulty register on e1ᵃ are written in their proper position. The 'Book of Coat of Armour' contains only one correction, which was followed.

In contrast the corrections in the 'Book of Blasing of Arms' are numerous. In this part of the edition it was apparently considered necessary to modernize, or render more acceptable to a metropolitan reader, the archaic or provincial spellings found in **SA**. Thus on c1ᵃ the following alterations were made, and followed by the compositor:

SA	W
ordant	ordeyned
mony colowris ther be	many colours there ben
needis	nede
bot	but
flowris	floures

war	were
cros	crosse
Dragonys	dragons
sheelde	shelde
waar	were
awngell	angell

Apart from the corrections thus indicated the compositor has made many other corrections of his own in the same direction; on c1ᵃ, for example:

SA	W
shewyd	shewed
a foore	afore
signys in armys	sygnes in armes
emonge	amonge

The only extensive verbal correction is the following, not followed by the compositor:

SA c1ᵇ,l.6 : I aske here moo questionis of the crossis signe

Correction : In askyng moo questyons of the sygne of the crosse

W ²a1ᵇ,l.1 : I aske here mo questyons of the crossys sygne

There are numerous instructions for amending the colouring or design of the armorial cuts in the 'Book of Blasing of Arms'. Thus against the four shields on the opening **SA** c3ᵇ/c4ᵃ is written: (1) the rondes most be yolo (2) this end most be as *the* other is (i.e. fleury) the cros gold (3) the cros gold (4) put in lityll blake or nō. These instructions have mostly been carried out in **W**, but occasionally ignored, sometimes rightly. On **W** a3ᵇ=**SA** c3ᵇ (see (2) above) the foot of the cross remains pointed, as it ought, for the text describes a 'crosse flurry fixabyll' (i.e. fitchy). On **W** a3ᵇ=**SA** c4ᵃ (see (4) above) the instruction is also ignored, and an error is made by exchanging this cut of a plain watery cross with the plain cross corded on ²a3ᵇ.

After press-editing the text was cast off to enable the compositor (or compositors) to set by formes. The casting off was probably done for each quire after the completion of the setting of the preceding quire. Casting off was performed by counting lines and noting the number of the future page within the quire in ink in the margin. The marginal figures (all in arabic numerals) therefore run from 2 to 12.

Where the text was in verse 38 lines for each page were counted off. For d6ᵇ 39 lines were counted off, and **W** too contains 39 lines. For prose (e6ᵃ onwards) 38 to 39 lines were counted off; for prose containing illustrations the number of lines was roughly estimated as 26 lines for a page with two large shields, to 33-38 lines for a page with three small shields. Any

The Book of Hawking, Hunting and Blasing of Arms.
St Albans, The Schoolmaster Printer, 1486.
Duff 56. Leaf ²d 1 verso.
British Library IB.55712.
Line 7 was cast off as ²b 1 verso (page 2 in quire ²b) in Wynkyn de Worde's edition of 1496.
The compositor indicated with which word ('the pro-pur') page 2 should begin after setting the previous page.

shall be sayd of him that berie theys armys in thys wyse as it
shall folow . first in latyn thus . ℂ portat vnam crucem er
reminalem . Et gallice sic . ℂ Il port vng croys ermine
Anglice sic . ℂ He berith a cros ermyn . And here ye moost
note that the coloure i theys armys shall not be expressid for this
cros ner theis armis may not be made bot of theys colouris that
is to say allone of blacke and white the which ar the propur colo⁹
ris of theys armys .

Sufficientli is spokyn of crossis afore . now folowig an odir
tretyse of dyuerse armys quarterydas here shall be shewyd.

Off armys quarterid sum ar armis quarterid playn Sum
quarterid engradid . Sum quarterid irrasid . Sum quar
terid inueckyd . Sum quarterid indentid of the which it shall be
spokyn euerich oon after other . and first of tharmys playn .

It shall be shewyd first of armys quarterid playn .

Three maner of wyse armys may be quarterid . The first
maner is opyn whan . ij. dyuerse armys ar borne quarterli . as it is opyn and playn in tharmys of the kyng of Fraun
ce er of Englond And ye shall say of hym
yᵗ berith theys armys thus as folowys. first
i latyn . Ille portat arma regis Francie er
Anglie quarteriata . Et gallice sic .
ℂ Il port lez armes de Frances et dangle
terre quarteles .Anglice sic . ℂ He berith
tharmys of France er Englond quarterli .

difficulties could be solved by the distribution of white on the page.

The last phase—marking by the compositor—can be distinguished by blind scratches apparently made with a dry point. When he had completed the setting of a page the compositor would mark the changeover with an acute-angled sign < linking the last line of the completed page with the first line of the next. When the break occurred within the line this would also be marked by a vertical scratch in the line. The beginning of each quire is marked with a scratched squiggle.

There are traces of one revision. Initially quire f was planned to contain eight leaves (sixteen pages) as appears from the numerals 2-14 that were noted in casting off. In this calculation an error was made in counting which caused the omission of page 3 of the future quire f. This mistake may not have been discovered until a part of the text was set since there are also numerals scratched in the margins which perpetuate the error. At some stage, probably when the error was discovered, it was decided to print two quires, f^4 and g^4, instead of f^8. The correct page numbers were now written in ink. The last three pages of g^4 were to be occupied by the beginning of the Treatise of Fishing. There is no indication in the printer's copy that the text of the Treatise of Fishing is to follow.

The compositor followed the casting off exactly for all the pages of verse, and a number of the pages of prose. In setting the other pages he deviated from the casting off sometimes by a few letters, sometimes by as much as three lines. None of the first pages of the quires were marked, with the exception of g. From the places where he was free to end his pages, implying that the following page was not yet set, and the places where he had to adhere to the casting off, conclusions can be drawn for the order of typesetting. For example in quire $^2a^6$ the end of

$a1^a$ (p.1) deviates from casting off	$a6^b$ (p.12) deviates
$a1^b$ (p.2) deviates	$a6^a$ (p.11) deviates
$a2^a$ (p.3) deviates	$a5^b$ (p.10) follows
$a2^b$ (p.4) follows casting off	$a5^a$ (p.9) follows
$a3^a$ (p.5) follows casting off	$a4^b$ (p.8) follows
$a3^b$ (p.6) deviates from casting off	$a4^a$ (p.7) follows

It therefore seems likely that the order of completion was pages 1-2-11-12; 3-4-9-10, or 3-10-4-9; 5-8-6-7, or 6-7-5-8.

A second example is quire $^2b^6$, where the end of page

1	deviates from casting off	12 deviates
2	follows casting off (title)	11 follows
3	deviates	10 follows
4	deviates	9 deviates
5	deviates	8 follows
6	deviates	7 deviates

The order of completion was therefore probably pages 1-12-2-11; 3-4-9-10; 5-6-7-8. It may therefore be concluded that the text was set sheet by sheet, working from the outer sheets towards the inner sheets, and that sheets were completed as soon as possible. Quire f^4, g^4, originally planned as f^8, is perhaps an exception. In view of the combination with another text, to be set from different copy, the outer sheets may have been left to the last, and setting may have started with the middle of the intended quire f^8, i.e. with pages 7 and 8, thought to be pages 8 and 9, etc., working outwards.

Changes made by the compositor in the text, without any editorial instruction, are numerous, for example:

SA $e3^b$,l.16: And of this ilke hare speke we no mare

W $d2^1$,l.1: And of this sayd beest to trete: here it shall be lete

SA $b5^a$,l.14: There be diuerse beryngys of feeldys

W $g3^a$,l.1: There ben thre dyuers beerynges of feldys

SA $b5^b$,l.15: Here endeth the mooste speciall . . .

W $g3^a$,l.26: Here we shall make an ende of the moost specyall . . .

Running over of lines occurs on $f3^a$ and $^2d5^a$. On $f3^a$ the compositor ended his page according to casting off (see **SA** $^2a5^b$, l.26). For $^2d5^a$ the printer's copy does not survive. On $h3^a$ the last line is not quite filled out with text, while $d5^b$, $f4^a$ and $^2d6^b$ have 39 lines; $g4^b$ has 37 lines. For $d5^b$ 39 lines were cast off by mistake and on $f4^a$ the compositor ended his page according to the casting off (see **SA** $^2b1^a$l.26). For the two other pages the printer's copy does not survive.

A Curious Copy of Sallust
Italy, late fifteenth century

NICOLAS BARKER

London

The object under discussion here was described by Alan Thomas, as always clearly and honestly, as follows:

SALLUSTIUS (Caius Crispus) DE CATILINE CONIVRATIONE. Manuscript on paper, sixty-eight leaves, written in a clear humanist hand in black and red, some interlinear notes in a minute humanist hand, some headings in yellow, spaces left for capitals. Catchwords written vertically in red at the end of each signature. At the end of several signatures a series of initials, whose meaning escapes me, on a fairly elaborate scroll. Some worming throughout, very bad worming at end, the last leaf preserved by mounting on gauze. Sm 8vo, 210 by 135mm, calf over wooden boards, the boards themselves badly wormed, some engraved metal catches, lacks clasp. Bookstamp of Falconer Madan, dated 1878, on first leaf, also bookstamp of A. G. & M. Hammond. Italy. 15th cent. £125.

The worming is, in fact, the first thing to strike you about the book. Silverfish or firebrats have destroyed all the leather on the backboard and the spine, and have made remarkable inroads, being partial to paste, into the inside of the boards, virtually destroying the paste-downs (a furniture beetle has made less extensive inroads into the text). However, all seven little star-shaped bosses, and four hasps, the fore-edge hasps lettered 'ave' and the tail-edge hasp 'S' (the head-edge hasp has gone), survive on the front-board; what remains of the brown tanned leather shows that tooling was limited to a plain fillet joining the little bosses, vertically, horizontally and diagonally. Only five bosses remain on the backboard, with a fragment of the pink leather clasp-strap on the lower fore-edge.

A more optimistic bookseller would have described the exterior as an 'unrivalled opportunity to study the structure of a medieval book'. This is, in fact, quite true: there were three pairs of bands, now clearly displayed so that you can see the sewing, linen thread over hemp cords, in good condition, and the entry points and grooves in the outer edge of the board are also clearly visible; the interstices between cords and board in the grooves were originally filled with a solid black cement-like paste. The head and tail bonds were similarly inserted, the groove running diagonally on the outer edge of the board for a good inch before being taken through to the inner and the cord frayed out and flattened under the paste-down.

The manuscript is written in a rapid but professional, if somewhat undistinguished, Italian humanist hand on paper watermarked with a posthorn (Briquet 7680 ff., which does not help to localise or date it) in quires of eight leaves. Although the margins are large and the writing area small (105 by 62mm, ruled lightly in lead pencil with the second line full across the page, but subsequent lines only ruled within the panel), it strongly suggests a copy from a printed book. I cannot really explain this, and certainly cannot substantiate it, partly because no editor of Sallust has collated the early printed editions and partly because the readings of the manuscript are substantially and exotically inaccurate, although (interestingly) these errors do reveal a sound knowledge of Latin, if slipshod in application. I think the resemblance is merely based on the similarity of paragraphing, of the relative size of initial spaces, and of the choice of letters for capitalization following the initial. I may be quite wrong, although there are easily enough of all editions of Sallust to make the surmise possible (nearly twenty were printed between the still unassigned, but probably Venetian, *editio princeps* of 1470 and 1480)

So far, it would be hard to imagine a more common-place object. But what struck Alan—I know, because he told me, though he was too cautious to make much of it in his description—was the decidedly eccentric rubrication and the frankly extraordinary scrolls at the end of the first, second, sixth and eighth signatures, which, with the final inscription, are in some sort of code that defeated Alan and has since defeated me. The rubrication, initially in red and green (originally, I think, not yellow), and then in red with occasional touches in the text ink, is more elaborate than one would expect in so plain a book. The capitals following the initial blank frequently run on to three lines, and are written with vigour and a sense of calligraphic possibilities that often destroys the regularity of the letter forms. The catchwords are regularly written by the rubricator running down into the tail-margin along the inner side of the inner bounding line, to be read by a binder looking in from the fore-edge. They are in the same decorative capitals as the chapter-rubrications, with one or more pairs of finials above and below the line for extra decoration. Words are often elaborately punctuated with stars or florets.

The concatenation of the inks used strongly suggests that rubricator and text-scribe are the same. Although the four scrolls seem rather more distinct from the writing of the pages on which they appear, the similarity of the code (if such it be) inscriptions on them and in the final inscription, which runs on after the end of the text, makes it pretty clear that the same hand was responsible for them too; altogether, the manuscript looks like a one-man job. As I say, the inscriptions defeat me, as they did Alan, and I can only set them out here in the order in which they seem to be intended to appear:

End of Quire 1: A.   A.I.   M.K.   C.R.   I.T.H
End of Quire 2: M D N   C I M O   O I R
End of Quire 6: A M C IV   DVLIA   ILA   I N V
End of Quire 8: P.S.   HI.   A. R. A. O. M./O. L./
(see Plate)   M.O.T.A.I. A. C.A.

The spaces between letters indicate the presence of a fold in the scroll. Unspaced letters appear next to each other on the scroll.

The final inscription, too badly wormed to be certainly recoverable, is as follows:

I should desperately like to penetrate the last inscription, which I strongly suspect conceals a signature and a date. And I am vastly curious about those odd scrolls. I thought at first that they might correspond to the missing initials in the preceding or succeeding quire, but not a bit of it. The section breaks are irregular, but none contains as many letters as are in the scrolls, nor do they correspond with the omissions.

Perhaps some more able palaeographer than I can solve this mystery. I live in hopes, and remain grateful to Alan for letting me have such a nice if unostentatious book, and for setting me a problem that continues to fascinate me, and which one day—who knows?—I may finally solve. To give knowledge and stimulate others to gain it is a great gift: it is one that, more than any other, has characterised Alan's work as a bookseller for half a century.

pugnadi no dare. Sperabat
prope die magnas copias sese
habituræ si rome soti icepta pa
trasse. Interea nutia reputa
bat cui initio adeu mag copie
ocurrebat q opibz oiurationis
fretus simlq. alienu suis ratioibz
existimas uideri cuz cuiui cui
fugitiuis suis omisicasse. Sz
postqz incastra nutius puenit
misceri dicens rome oiurationis
patefacta deletulo & Cetego ce
teris quos supra memoraui ni
ditui sumptu ce. pleriqz quos
adbellu spes rapinaz aut noui
aru reqz studiu illuxerat dilabuē

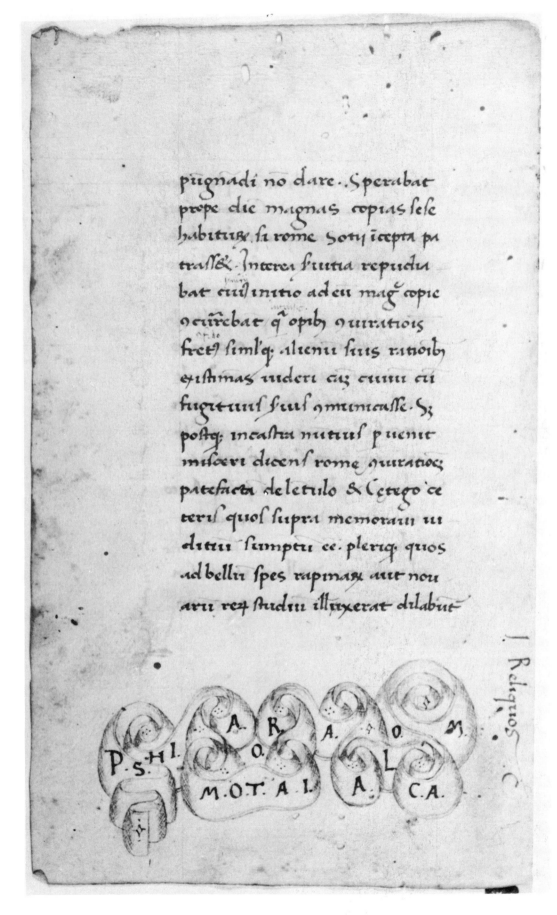

'De Catiline Coniuratione', end of quire 8, fol.64ᵛ, 210x135mm

Brant, *Stultifera Nauis*
Basel, 1497

CHARLOTTE and ARTHUR VERSHBOW

Newton Centre, Massachusetts

'I am the first foole of all the whole navie' proclaims the character shown in the opening woodcut, illustrated here, of Sebastian Brant's famous *Ship of Fools* (translation by Alexander Barclay). He is the book collector, dusting his collection of unread books, and the verses describe him mindlessly amassing quantities of volumes in fancy bindings, the possession and care of which give him much satisfaction, but little wisdom.

The *Stultifera Nauis*, or *Ship of Fools* (Basel, March 1497), one of the very earliest of our book purchases, and one of our best, came from Alan G. Thomas's first catalogue of 1957. We began as

collectors of prints, and only gradually were drawn into the enjoyment of illustration as part of the greater whole, the book. Alan's catalogues were always a delight to read, the stock of books, manuscripts and prints described with impressive erudition and at the same time, engaging wit. Of the *Ship of Fools* Alan remarked to us, 'Where else could a (print) collector obtain a set of 117 woodcuts by Albrecht Dürer and associates for £120?'

The first edition of the *Ship of Fools*, or *Das Narrenschiff* (1494), in German, is extremely rare. The blocks showed little wear by the time of the 1497 edition, however, and the copy which we bought from Alan has the woodcuts in very fine impressions. Of the 117, seventy or so have been variously assigned, in whole or in part, to the young Dürer. Wynne Jeudwine has pointed out that, though Gothic in style and technique, the cuts have a humour and insight into human nature that look forward in spirit to the Renaissance.

The book, with Brant's remarkable text matched by the masterly illustration, is one of the most outstanding and influential of its time. It was so popular that it appeared in more than fifteen editions and translations before the end of the fifteenth century alone, and in numerous versions in later centuries.

In the next few years after Catalogue One, we acquired a number of other books from Alan Thomas. A particularly fine one was the Pinder *Passion* of 1507, with splendid woodcuts made by Baldung Grien, Schäufflein and Kulmbach—a great book obtainable without much difficulty in the 1960s, but quite hard to find today. Another was the Estienne *De dissectione partium corporis . . .* (Paris, 1545), a beautifully printed anatomy book with imaginative woodcuts from the School of Fontainebleau. It was a fine copy, but with a few stains which Alan suggested might have come from use in the surgery!

These books are not only beautiful in themselves but have also opened up for us new directions in collecting.

The Aldine Aristophanes, Venice, 1499 and others

SIR KARL POPPER

Penn

4th March, 1981.

My dear Mr Thomas,

The news of your approaching seventieth birthday struck me as so improbable that I had to look again and again at the letter that informed me of it, because I was thinking, again and again, that my bad memory was playing me some tricks, and it must be the sixtieth.

As I thought of the beginning of our friendship, and of the most charming and indeed fascinating of Fine Books *series—your marvellous catalogues—it became clear to me that Aldus, your cat, played a most important part in it. For it was not so many years after my wife and I lost our unforgettable Chunky, a cat who made some very important contributions to my theory of knowledge. Aldus knitted a tie that has lasted well, strengthened by our common admiration for him and his tribe. Of the many productions by another Aldus and his tribe whose acquaintance I owe to you, the most beautiful is the volume of 1499, containing the first edition of the works of Aristophanes. Only a genuine diamond could remain so little affected by almost 500 years. To mention just a few other gems from Aldus: two first and contemporaneous pocket editions, in italics, of Dante's* Terze rime, *one prior and one posterior to the introduction of the famous Aldine Anchor-and-Dolphin. Two of Aldus's pocket editions struck me especially because I had used some (slightly inferior!) pocket editions of the same works many years before for teaching Latin: Sallust and Julius Caesar.*

It is pointless, of course, to remind you of the many beautiful Aldine first editions which you have shown to me. I only wish to mention one more: a Thucydides.

Years later, realising my interest in science and its history, you showed me a second edition of Newton's Principia, *almost if not quite as interesting as the first, and again as new as a diamond. It is possible that it was my enthusiasm when I saw this book—I think, the greatest in the intellectual history of mankind—which moved you to include science and its history among your subjects. Or was it my enthusiasm for the first edition of Galileo's* Dialogo? *I am afraid my memory may play me some tricks again. However this may be, I flatter myself that it was at least partly your thought of me and my amateurish enthusiasms which led to your decision to enter into a new field: science. You, in turn, introduced me to the first editions of some other great books: another Newton:* The Theory of Fluxions; *Leibniz's corresponding* Nova Methodus; *another Galileo: the* Discorsi; *and a few of the works of that wonderful and attractive personality, Johannes Kepler, from whose* Harmonice mundi, *chapter XII, I had translated and published a few years earlier one of the most beautiful passages on music ever written. In this passage Kepler starts by connecting the movement of the planets—his real topic—with the divine music of the spheres. Yet almost unintentionally he changes his topic and concludes with a hymn of praise to the music created by man—to the polyphonic music that was still a fairly recent discovery. Here are Kepler's words from the* Harmonice mundi *in my translation:*

Thus the heavenly motions are nothing but a kind of perennial concert, rational rather than audible or vocal. They move through the tension of dissonances that are like syncopations or suspensions with their resolutions (by which men imitate the corresponding dissonances of nature), reaching secure and pre-determined closures, each containing six terms, like a chord consisting of six voices. And by these marks they distinguish and articulate the immensity of time. Thus there is no marvel greater or more sublime than the rules of singing in harmony together in several parts, unknown to the ancients but at last discovered by man, the ape of his Creator; so that, through the skilful symphony of many voices, he should actually conjure up in a short part of an hour the vision of the world's total perpetuity in time; and that, in the sweetest sense of bliss enjoyed through Music, the echo of God, he should almost reach the contentment which God the Maker has in His Own works.

I wish you many happy returns of the day, and as much as possible of the contentment of which Kepler speaks.

Yours, as ever,
Karl Popper

Aristotle, *Organon*, Venice, *circa* 1500 and other Manuscripts

JOHN L.SHARPE III

William R. Perkins Library, Duke University

Long-time liaisons of mutual confidence and trust between an academic research library and an astute and knowledgable dealer in books and manuscripts benefit both the dealer and the institution. The library can measure the success of the relationship in the accumulated wealth of printed books and manuscripts which enrich the research resources; the same accumulated wealth of knowledge which has passed through the hands of a dealer, is in turn a measure of his stature.

Between AGT and the Library here at Duke University orders and books have been passing for more than two decades, while significant portions of several library collections have matured with his able assistance. Many classical texts in first and important editions, together with early and late Greek and Latin manuscripts, and biblical and theological volumes from the sixteenth and seventeenth centuries, on the shelves at Duke, are marks both of his interest and assiduity and of our long-time successful liaison.

AGT has supplied a number of Greek manuscripts for the Kenneth Willis Clark Collection of Greek Manuscripts in the Duke Library. No fewer than eleven of eighty-five Greek codices have come through the hands of Mr Thomas. All but two of them had been owned by Sir Thomas Phillipps: a copy of Cod. Reg. graec. 2742 in the Bibliothèque Nationale, Paris, by Richard François Philippe Brunck (1729-1803) of Strasbourg in 1769 (DUL, MS Gr. 69) and Aristotle's *Organon* (DUL, MS Gr. 30).

The Aristotle, written on 208 leaves, 275 by 195mm, by two scribes in a beautiful small Greek minuscule, is primarily by Damiano Guidoto of Venice, who was at work there about 1500. All the manuscripts which are known to have been written by Damiano came from the Monastery of San Francesco della Vigna in Venice (on this see Paul Moraux, 'Aristoteles Graecus: Die griechischen Manuskripte des Aristoteles, I', in *Peripatoi: Philologisch-Historische Studien zum Aristotelismus*, 8 (Berlin, 1976), 133-135). The Duke Library Aristotle came from that monastery and survived in the Holland House Library, despite considerable damage to that Library during the London blitz.

The remaining nine Greek manuscripts had been in the collection of Sir Thomas Phillipps. Several came to him after a period of residence in the Jesuit College de Clermont in Paris and in the library of Gerard Meerman in The Hague: Theodore of Studios, *Writings against the Iconoclasts*, a fifteenth-century paper manuscript of 176 pages, 322 by 238 mm (DUL, MS Gr. 40, formerly Phillipps 3083); a miscellaneous collection of the writings of Nicholas Cabasilas, St John of Damascus and Nilus the Ascetic, 201 leaves, 318 by 211 mm, on paper, from the sixteenth century (DUL, MS Gr. 50, formerly Phillipps 11609); and the compilations of the writings of two seventh-century ascetics, Maximus the Confessor and Thallasius of Caesarea, 39 leaves, 332 by 214 mm, on paper from the sixteenth century (DUL, MS Gr. 67, formerly Phillipps 11608). The latter two were also a part of the collection of the Duke of Sussex, the brother of George IV. Other former Phillipps manuscripts are 7758 (DUL, MS Gr. 41), 7760 (DUL, MS Gr. 42), 20984 (DUL, MS Gr. 48), 3899 (DUL, MS Gr. 49), 8408 (DUL, MS Gr. 51), and 4551 (DUL, MS Gr. 73). The last named, DUL, MS Gr. 73, is a fourteenth-century copy of the Homilies of Saints John Chrysostom, John of Damascus, and Gregory Thaumaturgus, among others, on 136 leaves of paper, 220 by 138 mm, written in a small well-formed hand by one scribe. It was owned by Giulio Saibante of Verona in the eighteenth century, then passed to Henry Drury of Harrow in 1824, Payne in 1827, and finally to Phillipps in 1829.

Another fine manuscript, a Latin text, is a beautiful fourteenth-century Italian copy of Jacob de Voragine's *Legenda Aurea* (DUL, MS Lat. 111). This illuminated manuscript on vellum, complete in 314 leaves, 220 by 160 mm, is written in brown ink in a rounded gothic hand with headings in red. The names of the months and the number of each leaf are written in large red letters and figures at the top recto of every leaf. The initials are in blue and red with penwork decoration in the contrasting colour at the beginning of every legend. The binding is dark brown nineteenth-century calf gilt,

Left: *opening leaf.* Right: *final leaf with Damiano Guidoto's colophon (lines 8 and 9), 275x135mm*

The Aldine *Rhetores Antiqui Graeci* Venice, 1508, and others

J. RICHARD PHILLIPS

Stanford University Libraries

In 1973, Alan G. Thomas issued his thirtieth catalogue, devoted to The House of Aldus and dedicated to a different Aldus, more feline than Aldine. The catalogue was of great interest to the Department of Special Collections here at Stanford University because of its strong interest in acquiring Aldines for the Morgan A. and Aline D. Gunst Memorial Library of the Book Arts. We acquired nine items from this catalogue alone, four of which are examples of Aldine Greek letter printing. One of the finest of these is *Rhetores Antiqui Graeci* (1508), volume one only (shown open), which has some extensive early annotations in two different hands. Evidently these marginalia prevented the binder from cropping the margins. The stamp of the Colonna family appears on several pages and leads to a hopeful connection between this volume and the family of Francesco Colonna, presumed author of the *Hypnerotomachia Poliphili* (1499), one of Aldus' most controversial and impressive publications.

Of the more than two hundred Aldines in the Gunst Collection, we have record of acquiring at least thirty-four of them from Alan Thomas. His descriptions—precise, accurate, often touched with humour, and always scholarly without being overwrought—have certainly encouraged us to respond to his offerings as far as our budget would allow, and to sigh with regret over those we have sadly had to defer. The growth of our collection of Aldines has been nurtured by Alan Thomas's continuing interest in Stanford resulting in that most satisfactory relationship of bookdealer and librarian working together to develop a stimulating research collection.

What a delight to acquire from one concerned dealer the *editio princeps* of Aeschylus, in which the *Agamemnon* and the *Choephori* are run together as a single work entitled *Agamemnon*, and the *editio princeps* of Sophocles, formerly owned by the Duke of Grafton and by Henry J.B. Clements. Other volumes from the Clements collection which found their way into the Stanford's collection through Alan Thomas are the 1545 edition of Appianus of Alexandria's *Delle Guerre Civili et Esterne de Romani . . .* , bearing the arms of the Duke of

---

[continued from page 40]

with cathedral panels in blind. The *Golden Legend* is further represented in the Duke collection through the work of AGT: both by an incunabulum, and by a fine example of the printing of Wynkyn de Worde. The incunabulum, *Legendas sanctorum quas compilavit frater Iacobus ianuensis nacione de ordine fratrum predicatorum*, was printed in Basel at the press of Berthold Ruppel in about 1475. This beautiful large copy has an interesting early provenance, described in five entries, beginning in 1544 in Lucerne and concluding in 1811 in Jena. Caxton's translation of the *Legenda Aurea* was one of the richly illustrated religious volumes that Wynkyn de Worde produced during the latter half of his career. Printed in London on the 30th [sic] of February 1521, the volume contains no fewer than sixty woodcuts, exclusive of five factotums and about two dozens repeats. Printed in black letter, this copy is preserved in a

remarkably complete state since all known copies of the work are incomplete or made-up. One of the most popular books of the day, the *Legenda Aurea* was printed eight times in all by Caxton and de Worde. The fine Duke copy is bound in a dark red morocco of the early nineteenth century with gilt spine panels and interlacing gilt borders on the sides.

Counting the many books which Duke has bought from AGT is one way of measuring his value to this institution. It is better, however, to sample his wares from among the numbers of volumes we have bought. His choices determined the items we would choose from, and they have always been good. This institution and those who depend upon it for research forage—whether in the classics, in palaeography, or in theology—will enjoy for generations to come the fruits of such a happy relationship between a dealer in books and manuscripts and an academic library.

The Rhetores Antiqui Graeci *(open) and other Aldines acquired from A.G. Thomas*

Sutherland on the cover, and Clements's copy of Giovanni Aurelio Augurello's *Opera* (1505). The latter is additionally distinguished by its binding by Derome le Jeune, the bookstamp of Cardinal Altieri, and having come from the Hamilton Palace Library. Add to these the 1591 edition of Gozzi's *Dello Stato delle Republiche . . .* with a two-page, priced list of Aldine books at the end printed as an integral part of the volume; the first Aldine edition of *Diversorum Veterum Poetarum in Priapum Lusus*, edited by Aldus' brother-in-law, Francesco Torresani, and considered by Renouard to be one of the most beautiful and rarest of Aldines; and the Wodhull copy of Giovanni Pontano's *Opera* (1505 and 1518), and the range and diversity of Alan Thomas's offerings to Stanford become apparent. Considering that the Pontano volumes had prob-

ably been bound by Roger Payne—for sixteen shillings according to Wodhull's note on the flyleaf to volume one—with Wodhull's arms on the covers, the pleasures of and interest in the Aldines from AGT transcend the printing itself.

Through his efforts to enhance our Aldine collection, Alan Thomas has provided Stanford faculty and students with some excellent primary source materials and a delightful corpus of correspondence filled with valuable information concerning not only Aldines but also the wide variety of other material which has arrived at Stanford over the years. Acquiring antiquarian and primary source materials for a university library collection would be nearly impossible without the aid of knowledgeable, committed bookdealers such as Alan Thomas.

Quintuplex Psalter
Paris, 1509

BROTHER DANIEL BURKE

La Salle College, Philadelphia

In 1977, La Salle College, Philadelphia began a collection of biblical literature to honour the memory of one of its students, Miss Susan Dunleavy, who had died that year in an automobile accident and whose father was a trustee of the school. The College had recourse to Alan Thomas as it began the collection, and among items acquired from him at that time was a copy of the *Quincuplex Psalterium*, edited by Jacques Lefèvre d'Étaples, and published by Henri Estienne at Paris on 31 July 1509. The volume is printed, as Mr Thomas described it, 'in black and red, with charming decorated line-endings, looking for all the world like a Kelmscott Press book, only better', and it is bound in English blind-tooled calf of about 1550-60, with two panels on each side formed by a pair of roll-tools. The Psalter has some historical interest as one of the first publications by the Renaissance scholars who were venturing into the comparative study of biblical texts and sources. This five-column edition with commentary is not, of course, polyglot in the exact sense: four of the versions presented are in Latin (Gallicum, Romanum, Vetus and Conciliatum) and one is Hebrew. The honour of being the first polyglot edition of a book of the Bible belongs to the Psalter of Augustino Guistiniani, with texts in five different languages, published seven years later at Genoa—discounting, that is, the single sample sheet of Aldus Manutius's *Triglot* that was promised as early as 1497 but never materialised. The Lefèvre Quintuplex Psalter, however, represents at least the first substantial step into the publication of comparative texts from different languages, a development which soon had its first significant climax with the magnificent Complutensian Polyglot of Cardinal Ximenes in 1522.

Of great interest too, especially for a Catholic college like La Salle, was the provenance of this copy: John Fisher, Bishop of Rochester, 1459-1535, canonised in 1936. As Mr Thomas described, the gilt edges are gauffered with the legend 'FISCHERE IOHANNIS RUFFENSIS EPISCOPI'. The inference that this unusual inscription indicated personal ownership and use by the saintly and scholarly bishop could indeed be supported from several directions. Fisher's reputation in Europe, perhaps greater than that of his friend, Thomas More, rested as much on his work with Scripture as on his sermons, controversial writings, or other theological books. His devotion, especially to the Psalms, has been amply documented (see especially Edward Surtz, SJ, *The Works and Days of John Fisher*, Cambridge, Mass., 1967, pp.114 ff.) and among his most important works is *This Treatyse Concernynge the Fruytful Saynges of Dauid the Kynge & Prophete in the Seuen Penytencyall Psalmes* (1508). There is also his lengthy Latin commentary on the Psalms, the manuscript of which, as far as I know, still languishes unpublished in the Public Record Office. Erasmus wrote to Fisher encouraging him to help Lefèvre who 'both admires and venerates you'. All of this suggests that Fisher, in the normal course of events, would be likely to have obtained a copy of Lefèvre's text, not only for his own use but also for the extensive library he was then collecting for St John's College, Cambridge, of which he was one of the chief founders.

But Alan Thomas goes beyond such general probabilities. He notices in the inscription the 'distinctly non-English' spelling of 'Fischer' and the preference of 'Ruffensis' for 'Roffensis'. These variations lead him to believe that the inscription was done in France and that this volume is thus a presentation copy for Fisher. Hence the mid-sixteenth century English calf binding probably replaced an earlier one 'of velvet or silk, the sort of de luxe binding, rich with embroidery, which we see in miniatures of the author presenting his book to a patron, bindings which have so seldom survived [and] . . . not surprising that it did not survive in a scholarly edition like this, especially in the hands of so devoted a Bible scholar as Fisher'. He then elaborates a suggestion made to him by Nicolas Barker: the volume may have been a gift of Étienne Poncher (1446-1525), bishop of Paris and Ambassador to England in 1518. By that time, Fisher was in the middle of a prolonged controversy with Lefèvre, nominally about the question of whether the Gospels were referring to one or three

44

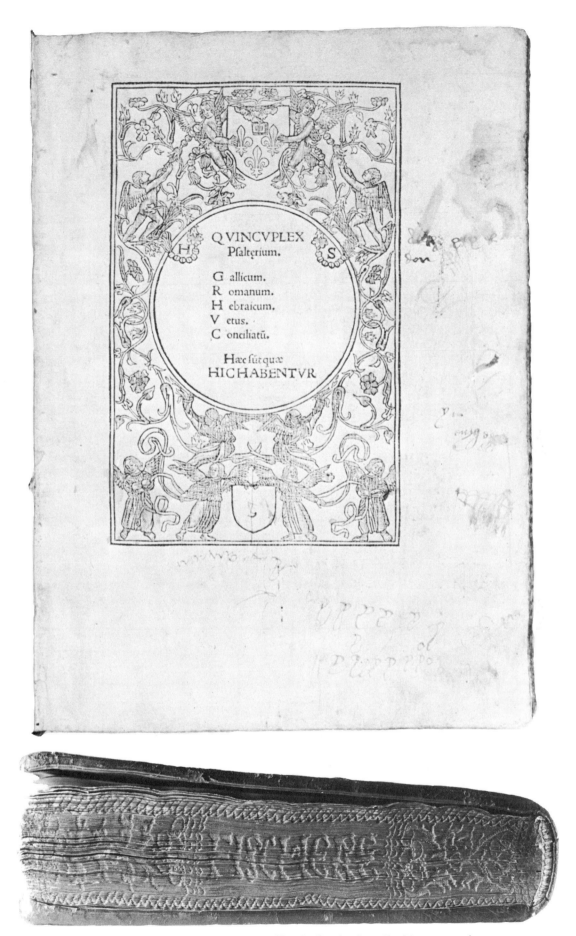

QVINCVPLEX
Pfalterium.

G allicum.
R omanum.
H ebraicum.
V etus.
C onciliatū.

Hæc ſūt quæ
HICHABENTVR

Top: title-page. Bottom: gauffered gilt edge inscribed 'FISCHERE'

French Book of Hours, *circa* 1535
A Problem of Long Division Solved

DAVID ROGERS

Bodleian Library

Over the years, a pleasant little stream has flowed from Chelsea to Oxford bearing parcels of various sizes and weights, more often than not deliciously chunky in shape. As in all the best-ordered streams, the current has been mainly in one direction, for Alan Thomas, at the source in Chelsea, has the unerring instinct of a great bookseller in becoming possessed of out-of-the-ordinary items which, once seen by a favoured client, prove irresistible. That is why so few of these parcels ever made a return journey from Oxford. After all, it is only in a very few libraries of the deepest resources that the questing scholar can hope to find early liturgies, for example, from all the far-flung dioceses and monasteries of Europe, in all their rich variety, and it seems to have been particularly among such liturgical books that the Bodleian has benefitted so happily from Alan Thomas's flair.

One such parcel, a few years ago, included an octavo volume modestly bound in eighteenth-century French calf. The sides were plain, the spine powdered with gilt fleur-de-lys except at the foot, where was stamped the date 1522 and what was evidently an owner's armorial device. A pencil note inside identifies this owner as Charles Paul Jean Baptiste de Bourgevin de Vialot de Molignoy, but it seems more likely that these are the arms of the family of La Mothe de Dreuzy—for most of us, perhaps, *ignotum* replaced by *ignotius*. Inside was a book-label printed in red, a monogram of the initials 'MT' in the style of an early printer's mark, which showed that this book had once belonged to Michael Tomkinson (1841-1921) many times Mayor of Kidderminster, writer on Japanese art, and member of the Roxburghe Club, whose own fine library was sold in 1922.

On the spine, a title-label proclaimed this to be 'Heures très devotes', words taken from a far from convincing pen-facsimile title-page, and the spine date of 1522 corresponded to that of an equally unsatisfactory pen-facsimile colophon leaf, claiming to be: 'Imprime [sic] a Rome . . . On les vend à Lyon en la boutique de Romain Morin libraire demourant en la rue Merciere.' Baudrier does describe a small number of books published by Morin at this address between the years 1519 and

[continued from page 44]

Maries in the passage about Magdalen, but actually about more general questions of scriptural exegesis and the authority of tradition. In one of three books that prolonged the controversy, the *De Unica Magdalena* (1519), Fisher mentions that Poncher had given him the second edition (1518) of one of Lefèvres books entitled *De Maria Magdalena . . . Disceptatio*. It seems natural, adds Thomas, 'that Poncher should also have given Fisher a copy of Lefèvre's most famous previous work, especially as he was encouraging Fisher to attack Lefèvre'.

After Fisher's execution, his great library was seized by the Royal Commissioners, trussed up in great casks, and the volumes carted away, 'besides a number that were stolen away'. Whatever its intervening history, the present volume carries a Latin inscription on the flyleaf, dated 2 June 1646, which asserts that the book then belonged to the lawyer, Richard Wythe, of Worcester, who had bought it from Robert Tomkins who had been given it by the late Reverend George Drumond, cleric. This may well, observes Thomas, carry ownership back to the sixteenth century. He adds that the Worcestershire connection is carried on by the bookplate of John, Baron Somers (1651-1716), Lord Chancellor, who played a considerable part in the Settlement of 1688 on the fall of James II.

I need hardly add that the present owners of the Fisher copy of Jacques Lefèvre's Quintuplex Psalter find Thomas's analysis of its tangled history a very attractive one. We also heartily endorse St John Fisher's words in his sermon on Psalm 101: 'Take hede what the importune and neuer seasynge labour in a grete & necessary cause dooth profyte & auayle. It is wryten *Labor improbus omnia vincit*: Incessaunt laboure . . . overcometh all thynges.' Fitting words are they not, too, for the long and distinguished career of Alan Thomas, Bookseller?

Suffragia.

noſtroʒ pōdere preminur/eius apud te
precibus ſublemur. Per chriſtum.
De ſainct ambroiſe eueſque antiēne.

O magnū ſacerdotē/birū ſctm ambro
ſium cuius fide ꝓ doctrina roboꝛata eſt
eccleſia:cui⁹ bita caſta fuit ꝓ oꝛatio pu-
ra:cui⁹ poſt moꝛtē anima migrauit ad

Woodcut of St Ambrose, 165x96mm

1543, but there is no Book of Hours of this or any other date among them. As for 'Rome' as the place of printing of an obvious 'Heures' in Latin with French prayers and rubrics, it makes no sense, especially as the handsomely bold and large black-letter typeface, and the style of the numerous woodcuts, mutely shout 'France' to us from every page. Perhaps the attribution to Rome was derived from the word 'Rome' which is found printed on the first leaf of each quire, but is in fact a catch-title which tells us that these are the Hours according to the usage of Rome.

Equally, with this impossible imprint, we should probably be right to dismiss the claim inscribed on the pseudo-title-page that these Hours were 'composed' by 'messire Iean Quentin'. True, this late fifteenth-century Paris penitentiary was the author of a book entitled *L'Horologe de dévotion*, but he was not the author of these traditional Hours of Our Lady, though brief tracts by him, especially his *Manière de bien vivre dévotement*, are to be found packed in among the various vernacular prayers in Hours of different usages printed at this period. These even include French-printed editions of the Sarum Hours, in which Quentin's opuscules appear in an English dress.

Clearly, the volume held what remained of a beautiful copy of a French-printed edition of the *Heures à l'usage de Rome*, but, alas, only a fragment. It was already in this condition when it belonged to another former owner who has not yet been mentioned, the antiquary and collector Dawson Turner (1775-1858). The start of an autograph note, written below his signature on a blank leaf at the front, runs: 'I nowhere find any account of this Volume, a portion of the leaves of which have been torn out and supplied by handwriting . . . '.

Besides the missing title and final leaf, several others had indeed been 'supplied by handwriting' and there were long gaps in the foliation. In fact, more than half the original thickness of the book had been made up with blank paper representing lost quires. Nevertheless it was with real regret that I took up this attractive remnant of a once fine book and prepared to have it parcelled up for return to Chelsea, with a report that I could not identify it further and felt I could not recommend its purchase by the Bodleian.

It had lain on my desk for many weeks, and a decision had become imperative. It was only at this knife-edge moment of impending rejection that, as I turned its pages for a final look, a subconscious memory suddenly stirred. Somewhere, at some time, I had seen another Book of Hours with the same kind of woodcuts and similar bold black-letter type. At home that night I rummaged in an old tin deed-box which held imperfect and unidentified books, and among them found a volume clothed in

an odious binding of crushed black morocco with gilt edges and shiny red endpapers, looking like an undertaker's hymnbook. Next day at work my own imperfect Book of Hours, for such it was, revealed itself as having indeed the same type, the same number of lines to a page, and a series of woodcuts, similar to the other. But more: not only did my pages match the Thomas ones typographically, but my volume began with a set of leaves foliated 34-47 and (after three missing leaves) ran on to folio 67 and, yes, the Thomas volume had a sequence from 1-33, then three odd leaves, and then continued from 68 to the end of the text.

At this point my fingers fairly flew through the jumbled collation which had so puzzled and frustrated my youthful understanding when I had acquired the book forty years before; now the pattern suddenly emerged at last. The longest portion of my book, 107 consecutive leaves, though bound last within my Victorian horror covers, actually slotted in after the calendar at the front of the Thomas volume, and exactly filled the gap in signatures between the calendar and his next leaf, which was foliated 108. The unbelievable was true: I possessed exactly what was missing from his book, no more and no less.

My purchase had been made, so my own pencil note inside revealed, on 26 April 1937 in Oxford, at the Turl Cash Bookshop (of blessed memory), for a sum which even in that pre-inflationary period was extremely modest. The splendid institution where I bought it (now happily once again a flourishing bookshop) was in those days the ultimate shore of Basil Blackwell's book empire. Thither were dispatched each week from the main shop in Broad Street sundry canvas sacks containing books which had not sold at the parent establishment. Prices were reduced accordingly; all transactions were for cash only (whence the title of this shop) and every term there took place a week's sale when the already reduced prices of the books in the Turl Cash Bookshop were all halved. So when, during my undergraduate days, Blackwell's acquired the remaining stock of the distinguished London firm of J. and J. Leighton, antiquarian booksellers of Brewer Street, there came about such a local glut of old books that it spilt down Turl Street also, and from the open window of the Turl Bookshop I was able to acquire treasures for which earlier, as a schoolboy, I had already developed a strong passion—bindings, early printed books and even incunables and manuscripts. My Book of Hours was part of the harvest of that golden age.

I fear that the gloomy binding of my volume must be laid to the charge of the owner whose autograph can be found within: 'Eadm^d· Waterton, Deeping Waterton Hall, Linc. 1884'. Learned and eccentric son of an eccentric father, he had sold his Yorkshire recusant family home of Walton Hall (where his father the naturalist had still climbed trees in his eightieth year) and had moved to an obscure Lincolnshire village which he believed had formerly been a Waterton family manor. He was a good antiquary and deserves to be remembered for his huge collection of editions of the *Imitation of Christ*, which was purchased after his death by the British Museum and became the foundation of that Library's matchless assemblage of the works of Thomas à Kempis in all languages.

In the end, of course, Alan Thomas's fragment never went back to him. It stands today on the Bodleian shelves, and beside it, sharing the identical shelfmark, is to be found its other half—my undergraduate trophy. Who could resist such a coincidence? My volume had to go to the Bodleian, which gave a generous price for it, and so the long division is over. Not all the secrets that lie behind that dismemberment have been revealed. As reunited, it—no longer they—still lacks seven out of its 232 leaves. Printer and date have still to be confirmed; it appears to date from after 1535, when the prolific Parisian liturgical publisher François Regnault issued from the Sign of the Elephant a dated edition of the *Heures de Paris* in which more than fifty of the same fine woodcuts were used, in much the same sequence, but showing in 1535 less signs of wear. About these cuts Dawson Turner, who was a discerning patron of the arts, had remarked (in the autograph note already cited) that one sequence of the cuts 'appears to be after Albert Dürer, or by the hand of some one of his school'. He was right; it was a Nuremberg artist, Hans Springinklee, a pupil of Dürer, whose monogram including the one of St Ambrose which is reproduced here.

The Whole Bible, Great Bible Version London, 1540

LORD WARDINGTON

Wardington Manor

While attending a lecture on Greek mythology in Lambeth Palace Library I found myself sitting next to Anthony Purver's Bible of 1764. It was in two volumes and I had never seen a copy before. But it was exciting to me, as the son of a Quaker, to see this Bible, the first attempt by an Englishman, a Quaker, to put the Bible text into the then modern and colloquial English; exciting too because, basing their lives on a moral code as preached in the Gospels, the Quakers required an understandable and modern text from which to live it. It was on an open bookshelf and I longed to take it down and handle it. That was in 1961, and very shortly afterwards I saw a copy in Alan's catalogue. This was my introduction to him and I bought his copy.

By far the nicest English Bible to come on the market recently was a copy of the 1539 Taverner's Bible in one of the Robinson sales. It was in superb and original condition and we decided to have a go for it. Alan was the underbidder on this occasion, but an export licence was withheld, funds were raised, and it is now happily in Lambeth Palace.

It was, I think, just after this that I was offered the Bible I describe below. I went to Alan's house to have a look at it, fell in love with it, and could hardly wait to get it home: *The Byble in Englyshe, that is to saye the Conte[n]t of al the holy scrypture, both of ye olde, and newe testame[n]t, with a prologe thereinto, made by the reverende father in God, Thomas arch-byschop of Cantorbury. This is the Byble apoynted to the vse of the churches. Prynted by Rychard Grafton. M.D.xl.* It is a copy of the second edition of the Great Bible and the first edition of Cranmer's Bible with his prologues. This is the first English Bible to have been officially appointed to be read in churches and to have this on the title-page. The edition represents Coverdale's continued revision-work on the text of the Bible, and shows the further influence of Münster's Latin Old Testament, especially in the Prophets, and of Erasmus in the New Testament.

The ten preliminary leaves are printed in red and black, and the colophon reads: 'The ende of the newe Testament: and of the whole Byble, Fynisshed in Apryll, Anno. M.CCCCC.XL. A d[omi]-no factu[m] est istud.' There are five title-pages, those to the Bible and New Testament being after Holbein and showing Henry VIII sitting enthroned and distributing copies of the Bible to the populace, together with Thomas Cranmer and Thomas Cromwell with their arms. The second title-page at Joshua, the third at Psalms, and the fourth for the Apocrypha, are each composed of sixteen woodcuts which appear in the text. The text of each title is printed in black and red. There are twenty-five woodcuts in the first part of the Bible (i.e., the Pentateuch), twenty-four in the second part, plus four larger initial letters to Esdras, Esther and Job, one woodcut in the Psalms; and in the New Testament, one larger initial to St Matthew and one to St Paul's Epistle to the Romans. There are therefore fifty woodcuts and six large initials in all.

The large initial 'P' at the beginning of the Epistle to the Romans contains the initials of Edward Whitchurch, and the title-page bears the name of Richard Grafton. Both had collaborated in the publication of the first edition of the Great Bible in 1539, and they continued to do so in the subsequent five issues of this edition. Most copies of this April edition bear the name of Edward Whitchurch on the title-page but this copy is the same as the copy in the Rylands Library. The April title-page also generally reads 'Archbishop of Canterbury', but this and the British Library copy have 'Cantorbury'. The mistake in Cranmer's Prologue has in this copy been corrected, and the initial at its head is flourished and not rectangular: again the Rylands copy is the same. It is possible and even probable that the title and Prologue in these copies have been inserted from the July edition, but this is perhaps not surprising as only a few months separated their publication. This copy from the Pembroke Library (Sn^2 shelfmark) was bound up in its present form in the early eighteenth century and has not been sophisticated and made up like so many copies in the nineteenth century. Signatures G and Iii as well as M$_{4\,\&\,5}$ are inserted from another copy, but a long time ago and possibly well before being bound in its present state. In spite of some minor repairs, a few small tears and some slight

Title-page, reduced

wormholes this beautifully printed and produced book is in excellent fresh condition and is generally very clean. It is bound in early-eighteenth-century English red morocco, the boards with a treble gilt fillet around the sides and the Pembroke tool in each corner, the spine very richly gilt in seven compartments, with gilt inner borders and gilt edges.

51

A Binding by the King Edward and Queen Mary Binder, London, 1552

MIRJAM M.FOOT

British Library

Alan Thomas's interest in bookbinding is apparent from his catalogues, most of which contain a section on bindings, and from chapter three of his *Great Books and Book Collectors* (London, 1975). The catalogues following the first Abbey sale of June 1965, where Alan Thomas bought lavishly, show a particularly fine display of collector's pieces. The confrère, quoted in Catalogue 17, who remarked that Thomas's 'descriptions of bindings sounded like over-rich cake', meant no doubt that, as well as the best bookseller's butter, a basis of wholesome solid fact and a number of real plums made up the rich, appetising, and tempting whole.

The facts, the result of most meticulous and persevering investigation, speak for themselves, and are clear to anyone who reads his catalogues. Of the plums I could mention several: the 1540 Basel Xenophon bound for Robert Dudley, Earl of Leicester, by the Dudley binder, now housed in the Broxbourne Library at the Bodleian (see cat.1,260; cat.3,303; cat.5,206; W.E. Moss, *Bindings from the Library of Robert Dudley* . . . , 1934, no.16; Howard Nixon, 'Elizabethan Gold-tooled Bindings' in *Essays in Honour of Victor Scholderer*, Mainz, 1970, p.234, no.3); a binding made by Marcantonio Guillery for Giovanni Battista Grimaldi, originally covering Bernardino Tomitano, *Ragionamenti della lingua Toscana* (Venice, 1545), now a remboîtage containing P. Giovio, *Gli Elogi. Vite . . . d'huomini illustri* (Venice, 1558) acquired by the University Library of Amsterdam (see cat.6,283; cat.8,226; cat.10,208; cat.13,225; A.Ṛ.A. Hobson, *Apollo and Pegasus*, Amsterdam, 1975, p.182, no.131); a beautifully tooled Claude de Picques binding on a Marlianus, *Urbis Romae Topographia* (Rome, 1544), from the Abbey collection (see cat.17,222); and, from the same source, Plutarch's *Opera* (Frankfurt, 1599), in a pair of volumes bound by Williamson of Eton for Charles Somerset with his initials and the date 1604 (see cat.19,139; cat. 21,151). Similar bindings for him are now in the British Library (C. 128.k.3), the Bodleian Library, Broxbourne Collection (see Howard Nixon, *Broxbourne Library*, London, 1956, no.55), and the Pierpont Morgan Library (PML 1113).

Another real plum, disguised as a rather tough and unassuming currant, found its way through Henry Davis to the British Library. Alan Thomas knew and liked Davis and described him as 'among the noble benefactors who have done so much for the great institution that we love' (*Great Books and Book Collectors*, p.82). The book itself is imperfect and at first appeared somewhat puzzling. The text, a treatise on the Eucharist written in French, dedicated to Thomas Goodrich, Bishop of Ely, by François Philippe, and printed on vellum in the early 1550s, is bound in brown calf and tooled in gold to a design common in both France and England at that time. The binding provided the clue for the identification of the book. It was made by the King Edward and Queen Mary binder (see M.M. Foot, *The Henry Davis Gift*, London, 1978, I, p.25, no.35), decorated with interlacing fillets painted black, fleurons, small flower tools, and a centrepiece consisting of a monogram formed by the initials 'TGE' surrounded by the motto SI DEVS NOBISCVM QVIS CONTRA NOS. The initials 'AK' have been added later.

It was tempting to assume that 'TGE' stood for the dedicatee, Thomas Goodrich Eliensis, and F.B. Williams's *Index of Dedications and Commendatory Verses* (London, 1962) led to that work where most profound bibliographical secrets are already in print: the revised *STC* 16430 is the translation into French by François Philippe of the new Prayer Book, at the revision of which Thomas Goodrich assisted, dedicated 'A tres reverend pere en Dieu Thomas Goodrik, Evesque d'Ely & Chancelier d'Angleterre'. A near miss, but *STC* 6003.5, a translation into French, also by François Philippe, of Thomas Cranmer's *Defence of the true and catholike doctrine of the sacrament of the body and bloud of . . . Christ*, sounded promising. The only known copy was described in great detail and illustrated in the Pforzheimer Catalogue (1, no.237), and this identified the Thomas-Davis book as *Defence de la vraye et catholique doctrine du sacrement du corps & sang de nostre sauveur Christ, . . . Translatée de la langue Angloyse en francoys, Par Francoys Philippe, serviteur de tres*

Henry Davis Gift, P.1303, 145x90x30mm

Révérend pére en Dieu, Thomas Evésque D'Ely, Chancellier d'Angletérre . . . Imprimeé a Londres par Pierre Angelin, 1552. The Davis copy lacks the title-page, C3 and P6-8, and has, as well as the irregular pagination noted for the Pforzheimer copy, a pagination giving p.62 in-stead of 64, 63 for 65, and so on. It consists, like the Pforzheimer copy, of 115 leaves—the faulty pagination accounts for that—but, unlike it, is printed on vellum.

W. Cole's *Extracts from the Registers of Ely*, IV (British Library, Additional MS 5827), has on fols 151ᵛ and 152ᵛ a drawing and description of Thomas Goodrich's arms with the initials 'TGE' and gives as his motto 'Si deus nobiscum quis contra nos'. It is more than probable that the Davis copy, printed on vellum and bound by a binder who worked for the Court, with the initials and motto of Thomas Goodrich tooled on the covers, is the dedication copy given to the Lord Chancellor by the translator who calls himself—not in the dedication but on the title-page—the bishop's 'serviteur'. According to Strype, Goodrich 'procured a learned Frenchman, who was a doctor of divinity' to translate the new Prayer Book (*Memorials of . . . Thomas Cranmer*, Oxford, 1812, I, 416), and R. Masters calls Philippe 'a dependent' of Goodrich (*The History of the College of Corpus Christi . . . Cambridge*, Cambridge, 1753, p.295). The coincidence that on 10 March 1552 the Lord Chancellor, 'by virtue of the king's warrant. For nothing because all the fees are pardoned by the Lord Chancellor's mandate', granted denization to 'Francis Phillipp' (Patent Rolls, 6 Edward VI, part IV [m.1]; his country of origin has been left blank), opens the floodgates for further speculation.

The Notes of the Geneva Bible 1560

CHARLES C. RYRIE

Dallas Theological Seminary

The one hundred and fifty editions of the Geneva Bible attest to its popularity, while the superiority of the translation itself makes all too obvious the deficiencies of its predecessor, the Great Bible. Its annotations, however, exerted more influence than is generally recognized and these undoubtedly deserve more attention than they have hitherto received. Long range, they did much to help make Puritanism both in Britain and America the strong movement it was. Although we do not know who all the translators and annotators were, they were led by William Whittingham (who himself produced a translation of the New Testament, together with explanatory notes, in 1557) and were influenced, if not directly aided, by John Calvin, Theodore Beza, Miles Coverdale, and John Knox. Though the notes include geographical and historical entries, many are directly theological, and that theology is unashamedly Calvinistic. Popular in England, and appointed to be read in the churches in Scotland, this was the Bible which through its notes taught exegesis to many for more than half a century.

More immediately, the annotations of the Geneva Bible played a large part in motivating the undertaking of a new translation, the Bishops' Bible. The Calvinism of its notes made the Geneva Bible unacceptable to the leaders of Church and State in England, and the high quality of the translation made the continued use of the Great Bible unacceptable. The result was a revision, under the leadership of Matthew Parker, of the Great Bible, which was known as the Bishops' Bible, published in 1568. The translators were directed to add no controversial notes to the text and not to express any preference when a passage might be interpreted one way or another. Though nineteen editions were issued, the Bishops' Bible was never authorized or widely accepted so that the annotated Genevan retained its popularity and influence among those who read it.

King James affirmed its influence by his remark, 'I have never yet seen a Bible well translated into English, and the worst of all . . . is the Genevan'. He was, of course, referring not to the quality of the translation but to the Calvinism of the annotations

which displeased him greatly and was responsible in part for the initiation of the King James translation.

Generally, the Bishops' Bible ridded itself of 'diverse prejudicial notes' (Parker's description of the Geneva in his letter to Queen Elizabeth) by simply omitting many of them. For example, there are roughly two hundred and fifty explanatory notes in the Geneva on Romans while there are only about seventy on Romans in the Bishops'. The Book of Revelations is even more startling: only five explanatory notes in the Bishops', yet both margins, inside and outside, filled with notes on almost every page in the Geneva (see plate). Examples of the kind of notes, with their strongly Calvinistic emphasis, omitted from the Bishops' Bible, are:

> Proverbs 16:4: So that the justice of God shall appear to his glorie, even in the destruction of the wicked.
> John 6:37: God doeth regenerate his elect, and causeth them to obey the Gospell.
> John 10:26: The cause wherefore the reprobate cannot believe (i.e., because they are not of Christ's sheep).
> Acts 13:48: None can believe, but they whome God doeth appoint before al beginnings to be saved.
> Romans 11:29: To whome God giveth his spirit of adoption, and whome he calleth effectually, he cannot perish: for Gods eternall counsell never changeth.
> Ephesians 1:4: The principall end of our election is to praise and glorifie the grace of God.
> Titus 1:2: Hath willingly, and of his meere liberalitie promised without foreseeing our faith or workes as a cause to move him to this free mercy.

Interestingly, all but one of the above New Testament notes are copied verbatim from Whittingham's 1557 New Testament (Whittingham has no note on Romans 11:29). Indeed this seems to be the pattern: the Geneva includes almost all of Whittingham's notes among the many new ones which were added.

The attempt to eliminate offensively Calvinistic notes from the Bishops' Bible did not totally succeed. Surprisingly, it retained certain notes from

THE ARGVMENT.

IT is manifest, that the holie Goſt wolde as it were gather into this moſte excellent booke a ſumme of thoſe prophecies, which were writen before, but ſhulde be fulfilled after the comming of Chriſt, adding alſo ſuche things as ſhulde be expedient, aſwel to forewarne vs of the dangers to come, as to admoniſh vs to beware ſome, and encourage vs againſt others. Herein therefore is liuelie ſet forthe the Diuinitie of Chriſt, & the teſtimonies of our redemption: what things the Spirit of God alloweth in the miniſters, and what things he reproueth: the prouidence of God for his elect, and of their glorie and conſolation in the day of vengeance: how that the hypocrites which ſting like ſcorpions the members of Chriſt, ſhalbe deſtroyed, but the Lambe Chriſt ſhal defende them, which beare witnes to the trueth, who in deſpite of the beaſt and Satan wil reigne ouer all. The liuelie deſcription of Antichriſt is ſet forthe, whoſe time and power notwithſtanding is limited, and albeit that he is permitted to rage againſt the elect, yet his power ſtretcheth no farther then to the hurt of their bodies: and at length he ſhal be deſtroyed by the wrath of God, when as the elect ſhal giue praiſe to God for the victorie: neuertheles for a ceaſon God wil permit this Antichriſt, and ſtrompet vnder colour of faire ſpeache and pleaſant doctrine to deceiue the worlde: wherefore he aduertiſeth the godlie (which are but a ſmale portion) to auoide this harlots ſlateries, and bragges, whoſe ruine without mercie they ſhal ſe, and with the heauenlie companies ſing continual praiſes: for the Lambe is maried: the worde of God hathe gotten the victorie: Satā that a long time was vntied, is now caſt with his miniſters into the pit of fyre to be tormented for euer, where as cōtrariwiſe the faithful (which are the holie Citie of Ieruſalem, & wife of the Lambe) ſhal enioye perpetual glorie. Read diligently: iudge ſoberly, and call earneſtly to God for the true vnderſtanding hereof.

CHAP. I.

1 The cauſe of this reuelation. 3 Of them that read it. 4 Iohn writeth to the ſeuen Churches. 5 The maieſtie and office of the Sonne of God. 20 The viſion of the candleſtickes and ſtarres.

1 THe ᵃ reuelation of IESVS CHRIST, which ᵇ God gaue vnto him, to ſhewe vnto his ſeruants things which muſt ſhortely be ᶜ done: which he ſent, and ſhewed by his Angel vnto his ſeruant Iohn,

2 Who bare recorde of the worde of God, and of the teſtimonie of Ieſus Chriſt, and of all things that he ſawe.

3 Bleſſed is he that readeth, and they that heare the wordes of this ᵈ prophecie, and kepe thoſe things which are written therein: for the time is ᵉ at hand.

4 Iohn, to the ᶠ ſeuē Churches which are in Aſia, Grace be with you & peace frō him Which * is, & Which was, & Which is to come, and from the ᵍ ſeuen Spirits which are before his Throne,

5 And from Ieſus Chriſt, which is a * faithful witnes, & *the firſt begotten of ŷ dead, and Prince of the Kings of the earth, vnto him that loued vs, & waſhed vs frō our ſinnes in his * blood,

6 And made vs * Kings and Prieſtes vnto God euen his Father, to him be glorie, & dominion for euermore, Amen.

7 Beholde, he cometh with * cloudes, and euerie eye ſhal ſe him: yea, euen they which ʰ pearced him through: and all kinreds of the earth ſhal waile ʰbefore him, Euen ſo, Amen.

8 I * am ⁱ * and * , the beginning and the ending, ſaith the Lord, Which is, and Which was, and Which is to come, euen the Almightie.

9 I Iohn, euen your brother, & companion in tribulation, & in the kingdome and pacience of Ieſus Chriſt, was in the yle called Patmos, for the "worde of God, and for the "witneſſing of Ieſus Chriſt.

10 And I was rauiſhed in ſpirit on ᵏ ŷ Lords day, and heard behinde me a great voyce, as it had bene of a trumpet,

11 Saying, I am ˡ α and * , the firſt and the laſt: and that which thou ſeeſt, wrize in a boke, & ſend it vnto the ᵐſeuen Churches which are in Aſia, vnto Epheſus, and vnto Smyrna, & vnto Pergamus, & vnto Thyatira, and vnto Sardi, and vnto Philadelphia, and vnto Laodicea.

12 Then I turned backe to ſe the ⁿ voyce, that ſpake with me: & when I was turned, I ſawe ᵒ ſeuen golden candleſtickes,

13 And in the middes of the ſeuen candleſtickes, one like vnto the ᵖ Sonne of man, clothed with a garment q downe to the

feete,

a Of things which were hid before. b Chriſt receiued this reuelation out of his fathers boſome as his owne doctrine, but it was hid in reſpect of vs ſo that Chriſt as Lord and God reueiled it to Iohn his ſeruant by the miniſterie of his Angel, to the edification of his Church c To the good & bad. d Which expoundeth the olde prophetes, & ſheweth what ſhal come to paſſe in the newe teſtament. Exo.3.14. e And began euen then. Pſal 89.38. 1.Cor.15.21. coloſ.1.18. Ebr.9.14. 1.pet.1.19. 1 iohn.1.9. 1.Pet.2.5. f Meaning the Church vniuerſal. g That is, from the holie Goſt: or theſe ſeuen Spirits were miniſters before God the Father & Chriſt, whome after he calleth the hornes and eyes of the Iambe, chap.5.6. In a like phraſes Paul taketh God, and Chriſt, and the Angels to witnes, 1.Tim.5.21.

Mat.24.30. iſa.3.14. iude 14. h They that contemned Chriſt & moſte cruelly perſecuted him, and put him to death, ſhal then acknowledge him. Chap.21.6. & 22.13. i Alpha and Omega are the firſt and laſt letters of the a b c of the Grekes. k Which ſome call ſunday: S Paul the firſt day of the weke, 1 Cor.16,1. act. 20,7. and it was eſtabliſhed after that the Iewes Sabbath was aboliſhed. l I am he before whome nothing was, yea, by whome whatſoeuer is made, was made, and he that ſhal remaine when all things ſhal periſh, euen I am the eternal God. m Of ŷ which ſome were fallen: others decayed: ſome were proude, others negligent: ſo that he ſheweth remedie for all. n That is, him whoſe voyce I heard. o Meaning the Churches. Chriſt the head of the Church. p Which was q As the chief Prieſt.

Revelation, p.1, reduced (reproduced from a copy acquired from Alan Thomas by Richard Linenthal)

The First Bishops' Bible London, 1568

JOHN WOLFSON

New York

Over the years I have bought many important Bibles from Alan Thomas—a first edition of the Great Bible (1539), a first edition of the Matthew Bible (1537), and a 1536 Tyndale Bible (the 'Mole' edition). However, the book that proved to be the most elusive was the 1568 edition of the famous Bishops' Bible. Darlow and Moule claim that 'in typography and illustration this is perhaps the most sumptuous in the long series of folio English Bibles'. It took ten years to find a decent copy.

The book is virtually impossible to find in good condition. The New York Public Library copy looks like a piece of Swiss cheese at the back it is so full of wormholes. Lord Harmsworth had several copies of the book, all of them incomplete at one end or the other. And there is no copy in the Pforzheimer Library.

Finding an unattractive copy was no particular challenge. Alan had acquired one rather inexpensively at a sale around 1970. I bought it by mail and when it arrived I was amazed to see that it lacked seven preliminary leaves which the auction cataloguer had neglected to mention. The catalogue contained the warning 'sold not subject to return', making no reference to its yellow edges, a parabola-shaped waterstain on two hundred leaves, and a shedding suede binding with a polished leather spine.

I felt initially that any copy of this book was better than none. However, as time went by I changed my mind. I did not have the book rebound; I did not have its margins renewed; I did not, in fact, do any of the things that one generally does to a book that one never expects to see a better copy of. I never brought the book home to the library, and kept it on a shelf in my office year after

[continued from page 54]

the Geneva Bible which were quite patently Calvinistic. For example, for 1 Peter 1:2: 'elect according to the foreknowledge of God the father', both Bibles have the same note: 'The free election of God is the effecient cause of our salvation, the material cause is Christes obedience, our effectuall callying is the formall cause, and the finall cause is our sanctification.' Calvin wrote that the efficient cause of our salvation is the mercy of the Father; the material cause, Christ's obedience; the formal cause, faith; and the final cause, the proof of divine justice and the praise of God's goodness (*Institutes*, III, 14, 17).

Occasionally the notes in the Bishops' even seem to be more strongly Calvinistic than the similar notes in the Geneva Bible. On Romans 9:15 the Geneva states: 'As the onely will and purpose of God is the chief cause of election and reprobation: so his free mercy in Christ is an inferiour cause of salvation, & the hardening of the heart, an inferiour cause of damnation.' The corresponding note in the Bishops' (at verse 11) said it this way: 'The wyll and purpose of God, is the cause of the election and reprobation. For his mercie and callying, through

Christe, are the meanes of salvation: and the withdrawying of his mercie, is the cause of damnation'. I would observe here that 'withdrawing of his mercy' is stronger than 'hardening of the heart'. Again, on Romans 11:35 the Geneva says rather innocuously, 'that is, provoked him by his good works'. The Bishops' elaborated: 'By this, the Apostle declareth that God by his free wyll and election, doth geve salvation unto men, without any desertes of their owne.' Perhaps the bishops were more Calvinistic than they realized!

One final, although not absolutely unrelated comment, in a humorous vein. How do Geneva Calvinists explain the rather embarrassing words of Christ, in the parable of the good Samaritan, which state that the priest came 'by chance' (Luke 10:31)? Here is their best effort: 'For so it seemed to mans judgement, although this was so appointed by Gods counsel and providence.' The bishops passed by their golden theological opportunity to comment on these words, probably because they chose to translate 'by chance' with the words 'it befell'.

Perhaps no theological system is ever characterized by total consistency!

year, waiting . . . waiting . . . I was never quite sure for what.

The last time I visited Alan it was with some apprehension, because it had been three years since I had bought a book from him for myself, and I was beginning to wonder if sixteenth-century books were finally disappearing from the market.

I arrived at Alan's door just as he was driving up in his truck. He waved to me as he got out, and walked away from his house, a few steps down the road. A flat wooden crate was leaning against a garbage can. Alan picked it up and brought it back.

'Sometimes my neighbour leaves boxes out here. They come in handy for packing large books.'

We went into Alan's book room. I fixed my eye on the shelves which were filled with Bibles, and I began to play my favourite game—identifying various books by the shape of their bindings.

'That must be a Geneva Bible over there.'

'That's right.'

'And what are all of those?', I said pointing to a row of six or eight very similar books; 'Douay Rheims?'

'Yes.'

'I'm sure the Douay Rheims Bible is the commonest *STC* book around.' Alan nodded. 'Do you have any idea why?'

'Probably', Alan replied with a twinkle in his eye, 'because the Protestants read their Bibles and the Catholics didn't.'

'Are those all "She" Bibles down at the bottom?'

'Yes.'

'And what's that next to it. Is that something else?'

'Yes.'

'What is it?'

'It's a Bishops' Bible.'

'Which one?'

'The first one.'

'What!', I shrieked. 'Where did you get it? When did you get it? Why didn't you tell me that you had it? Nobody tells me anything. I want to see it.'

We pulled the book off the shelf and put it on the table. It almost took both of us to lift it. It was in a very old binding, in very good condition, and had what ungrammatical collectors refer to as 'tons of margin'.

'I bought it at a sale at Sotheby's this spring', Alan said.

'I remember that sale,' I said. 'Where were you? I called you that week. There was no answer.'

'I was on vacation . . . '

'ON VACATION??!!'

'I left a bid with the desk.'

'That's wonderful,' I said. 'London's premier Bible dealer goes on vacation the day the first decent copy of the Bishops' Bible is sold in ten years.'

'I bought it anyway, didn't I?'

And so he had. And there it was. And at first glance the book had all the qualities which my own copy lacked. The size was ample, the binding was magnificent and the pages were clean. It was complete at the front except for two leaves, and one could hardly expect to do better than that with this particular book. And yet, with all of this in the book's favour, the price was remarkably low. And the reason that the price was low was because the last five leaves were missing. This was cause for celebration; the first Bible I bought from Alan Thomas, the book I found so unattractive that I had never even put it in my library, the most unattractive book I ever owned, finally, after ten years could do me a service. If there was one thing which this book, in spite of its faults, did have, it was leaves at the back.

Alan and I then spent the next hour putting our deal together. I would transfer the needed final leaves from my old copy to the copy which I was about to buy. A price for the new copy was agreed upon, and a trade-in price was agreed upon for my old copy. (Alan was always extremely generous in taking back books when I have been able to upgrade them.) Alan even agreed to see the new copy through the workshop of Bernard Middleton who would re-size the preliminary leaves, provide the necessary facsimiles, and construct a new and matching spine to give the book a truly magnificent appearance. All of this work would take a year. But by that time I had already waited ten years, and so another twelve months was hardly a consideration.

I remember leaving Alan's house that evening with three separate and distinct feelings: the excitement of having won what I considered a great prize, the elation of having achieved what I once considered to be impossible, and the satisfaction of knowing that in this twentieth-century world there was at least one other man who enjoyed, now and then, putting bits of the sixteenth century back together.

Scriptores Post Bedam
Edited by Henry Savile, London, 1596

SIR ROBERT BIRLEY

Somerton

RERVM / ANGLICARVM / SCRIPTORES POST / BEDAM PRAE-CIPVI, EX / VETVSTISSIMIS CODICI—/ BVS MANVSCRIPTIS NVNC / PRIMVM / IN LVCEM EDITI. WILLIELMI Monachi Malmesburiensis de gestis regum Anglorum lib. V. Eiusdem Historiae Nouellae lib. II. Eiusdem de gestis Pontificum Angl. lib. IIII. HENRICI Archidiaconi Huntindoniensis Historiarum lib. VIII. ROGERI HOVEDENI Annalium pars prior & posterior. Chron-icorum ETHELWERDI lib. IIII. INGVLPHI Abbatis Croylandensis historiarum lib. I. Adiecta ad finem Chronologia. LONDINI, / Excudebant G. BISHOP, R. NVBERIE, & / R. BARKER Typographi Regij / Dep-utati, Anno ab incarnatione, / CIↃ IↃ XCVI. (Before the Histories of William of Malmesbury, Henry of Huntingdon and Roger Hoveden are sep-arate title-pages, for the same printers and with the same date, but in the ornament of the title-page is the date 1574.)

We have here an excellent example of an important kind of book, a book of great significance when it first appeared, but which is now almost entirely forgotten. The publication in print for the first time of three of the works of William of Malmesbury, certainly one of the greatest English historians, and of the histories of Henry of Huntingdon and Roger Hoveden, did much to make the history of England in the Middle Ages a popular subject for study, not one confined to a few experts.

The book begins with a dedication to Queen Elizabeth signed by Henry Savile. He had been one of the Queen's Secretaries and, since 1585, Warden of Merton. In 1596, the same year as the publication of this book, she appointed him Provost of Eton. He was one of the greatest scholars of his time. But it has to be admitted that any modern student of these medieval historians would be ill-advised to use Savile's edition. There are many mistakes in his transcription. In fact, it has been suggested that Savile failed to revise the proofs of the book. Perhaps he was too busy becoming established at Eton.

There are, however, two more works of the Mid-dle Ages included in the volume now being con-sidered, and they are both very different. The Chronicles of Aethelwerd have a unique place in English history. He was a nephew of King Alfred and at the end of the ninth century ruled over a district of north-west Wessex. His Chronicles were largely taken from the Anglo-Saxon Chronicle and Savile used a manuscript which was more detailed than any other. This manuscript was destroyed in the disastrous fire of the Cotton Manuscripts in 1731, but it has been possible largely to reconstruct it from Aethelwerd's Chronicle. Savile, of course, had no idea of this. The Chronicle of Croyland (or, as it is now usually spelled, Crowland) was something very different and it may be regarded as one of the most splendid fabrications in English literature. Written in the fifteenth century, it purported to be the work of one Ingulph, Abbot of Croyland, who was Secretary to William the Conqueror. It came to be realised that some of the characters quoted in it cannot have even existed, but the narrative text was accepted until the nineteenth century when it was shown to be spurious. As late as 1883 a new edition was pub-lished accepting its authenticity.

The book is an extremely interesting one, but one must go further and refer to this particular copy. On the title-page is the signature, 'Lumley'. The book was in the library of John, the first Lord Lumley, certainly one of the first (if not the first) really large-scale private libraries in England. When he died in 1609, his library passed to Henry, Prince of Wales, and we shall have to consider him.

It may be argued that he was the most remarkable member of the Royal Family throughout the centuries of English history. He was born in 1594. His father, James VI of Scotland, became King of England in 1603. He was declared to be Prince of Wales in 1610. He died two years later in 1612 when he was eighteen years old. He was a constant visitor to Sir Walter Raleigh when he was a prisoner in the Tower and Raleigh dedicated to him the first volume of his 'History of the World', written in the Tower. Chapman dedicated to him his translation of the *Iliad* in 1611. He was on close terms with Ben Jonson. When he realized how poor Michael Drayton was, he gave him a pension of £10 a year. The first Catalogue of the Bodleian Library, pub-lished in 1605, was dedicated to him, when he was

Lower cover of binding, reduced

eleven years old. When he died many English poets wrote elegies to him, among them Donne, Webster and Thomas Campion (one writer has spoken of 'the mass of verse which Prince Henry's death occasioned'). He was in touch with Henry Wotton, the poet, the first notable English diplomat, and later Provost of Eton, who had the Prince's portrait in his room in Venice.

When he died, his library passed to his father and it became part of the Royal Library until this was given to the British Museum by George II in 1757. And then we find on the back of the title-page, and on the last page of the final Chronologia, the words stamped, 'MUSEUM BRITANNICUM' and 'Duplicate B.M. 1818'.

The magnificent binding in polished calf, with the Royal Arms and ornamental roses stamped in gilt, may well have been ordered by Prince Henry himself. If not, it cannot be much later than his death.

La Liturgie Angloise
London, 1616

LORD KENYON

Gredington

Over the years many books of a varied nature have come to me from the fascinating catalogues of Alan Thomas. They range from pamphlets to pontificals, and they even include an illustrated autograph letter from a veterinary surgeon at Market Drayton in Shropshire to the eleventh Viscount Kilmorey of Shavington explaining how he had been defrauded in the buying of a wagon horse upon which a surgical operation had been performed to conceal its broken-windedness!

The one which most touches the imagination, however, is a rather worn copy of *La Liturgie Angloise, ou le Livre des Prières Publiques*, printed at London by John Bill in 1616 (*STC* 16431). The volume shows much wear, with the title-page defective, the Catechism worn, the end-papers scribbled on and defective, and the two covers scratched and slit—every evidence of schoolroom use. On the blank verso of the last leaf of the preliminaries is the bookplate of 'James, [tenth] Earl of Derby, Lord of Man and ye Isles. 1702' (see plate). It is the early marks of ownership scribbled on the end-papers, though, which are of the greater interest: possession by at least one of the children of James, seventh Earl of Derby (1607-1651) and his wife Charlotte (1599-1664), second child and eldest daughter of Claude de la Trémoille, Duc de Thouars, by Charlotte (1580-1626), third daughter of William the Silent, Prince of Orange, and his third wife Charlotte de Bourbon.

At his death in 1604 at the age of thirty-nine, the Duc had expressed a desire that his children be brought up in the reformed religion. This was faithfully observed as is witnessed by a letter from Charlotte, at age five or six, telling her mother that she knew already seventeen psalms by heart. Her mother was often absent in Holland during Charlotte's upbringing at Thouars, and in 1625, when she came to England in the train of Henrietta Maria upon her marriage to Charles I, she took the opportunity to arrange her daughter's marriage to James Stanley, Lord Strange, later to become the seventh Earl of Derby, and heir to vast estates in Lancashire, Cheshire, and North Wales, and to the Lordship of Man. The wedding took place on 26 June 1626, the bridegroom then only twenty years old, some eight years younger than the bride. By August 1627, they had set up home at Lathom House and their family began to appear, the firstborn a son, Charles, who was followed by four brothers and three sisters, of whom one girl and two boys failed to survive infancy.

For the first sixteen years of their married life, Lord and Lady Strange lived quietly with their large family at Lathom House or at Knowsley. At the outbreak of the Civil War, however, the Earl adopted the Royalist cause and left to join the King. During her husband's frequent absences, the Countess led a spirited defence of Lathom House in a county which was for the most part favourable to the Parliamentary cause. By May 1643, Lathom was the only place in the county still held 'for the King'. Following the defeat at Marston Moor on 2 July 1644, however, the family withdrew to Castle Rushen on the Isle of Man. Lathom House was finally surrendered and dismantled with such success that not a vestige now remains. The family remained at Castle Rushen, refusing to make peace with Parliament while hospitably entertaining Royalists, until August 1651 when the Earl decided to join Charles II in his march through England. He was present at the Battle of Worcester and escorted Charles to Boscobel, but was soon after captured and brought before a court martial in spite of a petition to Parliament supported by Cromwell, and an open recommendation to his wife to surrender the Isle of Man. The Earl was removed from Chester to Bolton for safety and executed there on 15 October 1651. The surrender of the Isle of Man followed, and Charlotte, Countess of Derby, was allowed to leave with her family for Knowsley where she lived until her death on 21 March 1663.

Turning now to the scribblings on the end leaves of the prayer book, we find that the most numerous references are to the second but oldest surviving daughter of James and Charlotte, Henrietta Maria, born 16 November 1630, who married, on 27 September 1654, William Wentworth, second Earl of Strafford, KG. She died—childless—on 27 December 1685, and was survived by her husband

Bookplate and details of ownership inscriptions

Book-Sale Catalogues
from the Evelyn Library, 1682-92

JOHN BIDWELL

William Andrews Clark Memorial Library, UCLA

John Evelyn, translator of Naudé's *Advis pour dresser une bibliothèque (1661)*, cautions collectors of massive tomes and of sets in many volumes against

> neglecting in the mean time to procure and furnish themselves with an infinity of little Books. . . . Otherwise, it ordinarily comes to pass, that whilst we despise these little Books, which appear onely as mean baubles, and pieces of no consideration, we happen to lose a world of rare collections, and such as are sometimes the most curious pieces of the whole Library.

Taking this advice to heart, the Clark Library has acquired—whenever at all possible—pamphlets, broadsides and manuscript ephemera of the late seventeenth and early eighteenth centuries. To Alan Thomas's efforts and expertise, we owe such baubles as a broadside attack on the Quakers, apparently unrecorded; an open letter to the imprisoned regicides in 1662, one of two known copies; and the manuscript meteorological journal of Thomas Barker, eighteenth-century authority on comets.

We are particularly grateful for our set of seventeenth-century book-sale catalogues from the Evelyn Library, which Alan obtained for us despite frustrating delays and confusions at customs. They were worth the wait. In this one volume, we have, we think, eight catalogues dating from 1682 to 1692, all complete except for one lacking its title-page, and two fragments as yet unidentified. According to Wing and to Munby & Coral, two are the only copies in America, and three, perhaps four, are held by only one other American library. Some of the credit for their survival must go to William Upcott, who found them stashed among the Evelyn books at Wotton, appropriated them, and had them bound together in 1819. Upcott, of course, is now known to have been primarily responsible not just for the first edition of the Evelyn diary but also for large gaps in the Evelyn library. In this case, at least, he felt guiltless enough to note on a flyleaf that the catalogues were from Wotton and that he took them.

Upcott also observed that the catalogues were marked by Evelyn himself. In five of them nearly a hundred items were checked off in pencil. From his own inscription, we know that Evelyn bought at least one book at auction as late as 1689 and that in the same year *an* Evelyn was present for a sale on the 8th of May and there picked up our copy of *Bibliotheca Selectissima* (Wing B-2856; see plate). But we have found no direct evidence linking these annotations to the book-collecting interests of John Evelyn the diarist and author of *Sylva*.

At the time of these sales, Evelyn was in his sixties and early seventies, perhaps more interested in cataloguing his library than in building it. When

───◦◉◦───

[continued from page 60]

who died in 1695.

As in all such worn and ill-treated volumes, the imagination is led to scenes of nursery life: the learning of the Psalms by heart, the seemingly endless repetition of the Catechism, and so forth. In this case these were likely the first steps in learning an unfamiliar and unwelcome foreign language; even though it was one's mother's native tongue. This little volume serves also to conjure up a picture of domestic life at Lathom House, contained by encircling Parliament troops, or at Castle Rushen in the Isle of Man, where the news was so long in coming that the war seemed ages away. Henrietta Maria, caught sight of here in the nursery, was her father's favourite, and well she might be if there is truth in the scribbled verse on the last endpaper (see plate):

> Je suis á madame marie
> Dont la beauté est si accomplie
> quelle n'a point d'eguale dans tout cest univers oreille
> Elle á le teint charmant et la bouche vermeille
> le Corps fort bien formé et les yeux sans pareils
> Et bien apres cela nest ce pas une merveille.

BIBLIOTHECA SELECTISSIMA

SEU

CATALOGUS

VARIORUM,

Infignium, Rariffimorumque in omni Facultate, & Lingua Librorum, *viz.* Theologicorum, Medicorum, *fed precipue* Philologicorum, Rerumque Britannicarum Hiftoriæ Scriptorum, magna ex parte nitidiffime Compactorum.

Quos Magnis Impenfis & Summa diligentia fibi Procuravit quidam Angliæ *GENEROSUS* nuper defunctus.

Quorum *AUCTIO* Habebitur *Londini* in Vico vulgo Dicto *Ave Mary Lane* apud Domum dictam *Sams Coffee-Houfe,* Octavo die Menfis *Maii,* 1689. *This for Efq Enofin/ profent*

Per *JOH. BULLORD* Bibliop. *Londin.*

Catalogues are diftributed Gratis at Mr. *Henfmans* in *Weftminfter-Hall,* Mr. *Notts* in the *Pel-Mel,* Mr. *Browns* without *Temple-Bar,* Mr. *Batemans* in *Holburn,* *John Bullords* in St. *Pauls Church-Yard,* Mr. *Eddows* in the *Piazza* under the *Royal Exchange,* Bookfellers; and at the Place of Sale.

Book-Sale Catalogue, 8 May 1689

he moved his books from Sayes Court to more restricted quarters at Wotton, he cheerfully sold off the overflow, some 1,500 volumes.

But Evelyn bibliomania passed undiminished to the next generation. John Evelyn Jr confessed to his father, 'I was ever guilty of loading myself with books, and you will easily conjecture from whom I derive this laudable infirmity . . .'. And indeed, during these years, young John was a much more likely browser of book-sale catalogues than his father. He was at the right place at the right time to attend the sales, living conveniently near London under his father's roof at Sayes Court, and then in the city itself when he left home to study law. Perhaps it was with possible textbooks in mind that he obtained our *Curious Collection of Law-Books, Ancient and Modern* (Wing C-5370) and checked off William Rastell's *Colleccion of Entrees, of Declaracions, Barres, Replicacions, Reioinders, Issues, Verdits* (*STC* 20730) in another catalogue.

Our latest sale catalogue is dated 25 January 1692. Just a few months later, young John fell seriously ill, and almost immediately upon his recovery he left for Ireland where he had been appointed a Commissioner of the Revenue.

John Evelyn Jr was often indisposed. Seeking relief from ailments—and debts—he returned to England in 1696, and there he died in 1699. When his son's books were brought back from Ireland, Evelyn Sr proposed 'to purge out many frivolous French books and other trash . . .'. Young John, it would seem, had interests in law and in French literature not at all shared by his father. When it came to trimming the Sayes Court library down to Wotton size, his French and law books were, Evelyn thought, the most expendable. His son had defended both collections in 1693. He detested the

French as much as any loyal Englishman could, young John protested, but he 'always delighted in their language, and loved to read good sense clothed in it'. If his books were to go up for sale, it would be to sacrifice them to his debts: 'I fear they will more need Millington's eloquence when the inexorable £6 per cent brings them, and the rest of my poor movables *sub hasta.*' In *John Evelyn and his Family Circle* (1955), incidentally, W.G. Hiscock interpreted this as an allusion to Gilbert Millington the regicide. Would not Edward Millington the auctioneer be a better candidate?

The 'Esq. Evelin' who annotated *Bibliotheca Selectissima* definitely had a predilection for French books, frivolous or otherwise. Altogether twenty-six of them were checked off: political tracts, histories, prose romances, and above all, classics in translation. The Quintus Curtius Rufus, *De la vie et des actions d'Alexandre le Grand* (Paris, 1668), would have been of special interest to John Evelyn Jr, who had translated Plutarch's life of Alexander in 1685. In other catalogues, editions of Quintus Curtius in English (1687) and in Latin (1678) were also marked, along with the Plutarch to which Evelyn Jr contributed. Possibly young John was noting books already in the family library rather than desiderata. He surely did not need another Plutarch, nor for that matter his father's *Of Liberty and Servitude* (1649) or Sprat's *History of the Royal-Society* 1667, which are likewise annotated. But these are problems that cannot be resolved without examining Evelyn's own manuscript catalogue of the library as it stood in 1687. In the meantime, if we cannot venture anything more than these speculations on how and why the book-sale catalogues came into the Evelyn Library, we can at least express pleasure at how they came into ours.

The Gospels of King Iyasu II of Ethiopia Gondar, 1730-55

BENT JUEL-JENSEN

Oxford

Gondar had for centuries been the capital of Ethiopia, but the Emperor Tewodros decided to make a 'new Gondar' at Debre Tabor. He took 981 manuscripts from Gondar itself before setting fire to its churches (see *Chronique de Theodros II*, edited by C. Mondon-Vidailhet, Paris, c.1904, p.22), but in turn moved the manuscripts with his other valuables to his mountain fortress at Maqdala for safety. Lieutenant (later General, Sir) William Stephen Lockhart was aide-de-camp to Brigadier Merewether who joined Napier's expedition to Ethiopia to free the British captives imprisoned at Maqdala by Tewodros. Elephants, heavy guns, all sorts of supplies and 12,000 men were landed at Zula on the Red Sea in October 1867 and, after an incredible march through some of the wildest mountains in the world, they assaulted and took Maqdala on 13 April 1868. Tewodros committed suicide (see D. Bates, *The Abyssinian Difficulty*, Oxford, 1979).

Tewodros's treasure, including his library, was put up for auction on 20 and 21 April, 'some things going fabulously high'. Equipped with £1000, Richard R. Holmes, Assistant at the British Museum, bought shrewdly and brought some 350 manuscripts back, with one stroke making the Museum's Ethiopic collection the finest anywhere. Some 600 manuscripts were given back to the Ethiopians at Chalaqot, but a good many were probably bought by members of the expedition with antiquarian tastes. In an excellent article, 'The Library of Emperor Tewodros II at Maqdala (Magdala)' (*Bulletin of SOAS*, 1973, pp.15-42), Rita Pankhurst attempted to account for the subsequent fate of the manuscripts. Apart from those in the British Library, some are in Bodley and at Cambridge, the Queen has six very fine ones, and one only (untraced) was thought to be in private hands. This is an underestimate. At least five of my Ethiopic manuscripts were brought back from Maqdala by British officers. Alan Thomas got me Captain Sturt's little *Gospel of St John*, which had later passed through the Phillipps library. But whilst that was easily portable in its little book bag, Lieutenant Lockhart's purchase was quite

different. He acquired a magnificent *Four Gospels*, so large—440 by 380mm—and heavy—29·5lbs—that I would defy any man to carry it for more than a few minutes without being exhausted. He must have had a mule or a donkey to carry that alone back to Annesley Bay. On 9 July 1979 it was put up for sale at Sotheby's.

Over the years I had acquired some of the texts essential for a small Ethiopic library, but I had no *Four Gospels*. Somebody with some knowledge of Ge'ez (Ethiopic, the classical language of Ethiopia) must have catalogued it, for the mysterious and tentative date, 1730-55, was given without any explanation of this choice, and the illustration chosen had a prayer for King Iyasu and the (dowager) Queen Wolete Giyorgis. The dates are those of the reign of Iyasu II. Alan and I conferred. How much? Sotheby's estimate seemed much too conservative, and we settled for a limit well into four figures (a bid I really could not afford) with little hope of success. Alan rang me immediately after the sale, obviously shaken and delighted. 'I got it for £***!' (a sum only half Sotheby's higher estimate). A few days later the Thomases came in their dormobile with the manuscript. The car had only just made it, the springs had been groaning.

On closer examination the book lived up to all expectations. It is a regal manuscript written in a beautiful, mostly very large hand and in two columns. My Ethiopian brother, Leul Ras Mangashia Seyoum, a fine Ge'ez scholar and connoisseur of manuscripts, approved of it. He pointed out that it was written on horse vellum, a material used for very large books in Ethiopia. At the head of the

opening page is ወንጌለ፡ ዘፋድስ፡ መድኃኔ፡ዓለም፡ 'The

Gospels of [the Church of] our Lord the Saviour of the World', one of two churches in Maqdala. Some of the finest manuscripts from Maqdala have similar inscriptions, apparently in the same hand, including the magnificent *Tekle Haymanot* (late eighteenth century) in Bodley, and the *Life and Miracles of St Giyorgis* (early eighteenth century) in my own library.

We know who wrote the *Gospels* for the scribe has signed some signatures: ሀ ወለ ደ፡ ያ ዎ ት፡ Wolde Dawit.

There can be little doubt that the manuscript was written for King Iyasu, who may have given it to one of the Gondar churches. Details of church property were noted in blank spaces and one such entry starts impressively, 'I Yosab am on the courtyard of the King, of the Echege and all the Dignitaries, and I am head of Monasteries . . . ', and Yosab's seal and Arabic inscription appear in two places. The manuscript is bound in quite typical contemporary goatskin over wooden boards, boards, with characteristic doublures with a central square of oriental patterned cloth. The sides are decorated with blind tooling, including a central cross, a traditional style that has been used for centuries. Even my *Enoch* (completed and bound for me in Tigray by Archbishop Yohannes's scribe in 1974) has such decoration.

No one can collect books in an obscure field without the help of an intelligent and tolerant bookseller friend. I got attacked by *morbus ethiopicus*, an incurable disease, incomprehensible to some of my more conventional book-collecting friends who wince when I produce a recently acquired incense-smelling treasure. Not so Alan, who shares my enthusiasm. Ahmed Gran, 'the left-handed', overran Ethiopia in religious fervour in the early sixteenth century and destroyed churches and burned manuscripts. There has been no comparable disaster until the barbarians invaded the country in recent years and, supporting Mengistu Haile Maryam, began to burn churches and books, imprison, torture and murder innocents. Because of this, it is so much more important to preserve outside Ethiopia evidence of a great civilization for the young who must return when the alien forces are driven out.

Alan, your Ethiopian book collector sends his felicitations on your seventieth birthday, and looks forward to writing again in ten years' time.

ብኪራተ፡ኤቡ፡ቅሩፍ፡
ሉቃከ፡ወንጌሳዊ፡አ
ሐዱ፡እምስብዓ፡ወከ
ልኤቱ፡አርድእት
ጸሎቱ፡ወበረከቱ፡የ

ሀሉ፡ምከለ፡ንጉሠ፡
ኢየሱ፡ወንግሥትነ፡
ወለተ፡ጊዮርጊከ፮ለ፪
ለመ፡ዓለም፡አሜን
ወአሜን

እከመ፡ብዙኃን፡እለ፡
አንዙ፡ይውጥኑ፡ወይ
ንግሩ፡ወይምህሩ፡ሠ
ርዓተ፡ዜና፡ግብር፡ዘ
ንሐነ፡ጠየቅናሁ፡በእ
ንተ፡ግብር፡ዘአምኑ
በላዕሌነ፡በከመ፡አይ
ድዉን፡እልከቱ፡እሉቀ
ደሙን፡ርእዮቶ፡ወተ
ልእክም፡ለቃለ፡ፈቃድ

ከሊታኒ፡ረትዓኒ፡ከዐ
በከመ፡እጽሐፍ፡ለከ
እከመ፡ዐንከ፡እተልፀ
ለኰሉ፡ግብር፡በጥይቅ
ና፡እእዚዝ፡ታእፌሳፊ
ከመ፡ታእምር፡ኀይለ፡
ነገር፡ዘተምህርከ፡ኪ
ያሁ፡ወከነ፡በመዋለ፡
ሄሮድከ፡ንቱሠ፡ይሁ
ዳ፡ወህሉ፡አሐዱ፡ብ

The Gospels of King Iyasu II, St Luke, p.1, 440x380mm

A Leaf from William Blake's *America* London, *circa* 1793

RAYMOND LISTER
Cambridge

Alan Thomas has helped my wife and me to make three major additions to our William Blake collection. Some fifteen or sixteen years ago he sold us a hitherto unrecorded and fragmentary copy of an early issue of *Songs of Innocence* (now copy X in *Blake Books* by G.E. Bentley Jr, 1977); this has several interesting features which include an impression of 'Infant Joy' with the flowers coloured blue instead of the more usual red. Some time after this we acquired from him a beautifully crisp copy, in the original pink sheepskin binding, of Robert John Thornton's *The Pastorals of Virgil, with a Course of English Reading adapted for Schools* (1821), which contains Blake's only wood engravings. And just over a year ago we were lucky enough to add another item from an Alan Thomas catalogue, a splendid impression of plate 5 of *America, a Prophecy*.

The leaf contains this passage from the poem:

> Albions Angel stood beside the Stone of night, and saw
> The terror like a comet, or more like the planet red
> That once inclos'd the terrible wandering comets in its sphere.
> Then Mars thou wast our center, & the planets three flew round
> Thy crimson disk; so e'er the Sun was rent from thy red sphere;
> The Spectre glowd his horrid length staining the temple long
> With beams of blood; & thus a voice came forth, and shook the temple

The surrounding design is generally accepted to be a representation of the Last Judgement. At the top, in the centre, is a male figure standing on a cloud, his left leg is stretched and his right leg is flexed and resting on a higher part of the cloud. His shoulders are bent forward and his arms support on them a bound figure which he is preparing to hurl into the flames at the bottom of the design. To the left is a flying figure holding in his right hand a balance of justice, heavily weighted to one side; to the right is another flying figure, viewed from behind, who is carrying a huge flaming sword, probably symbolising retribution. At the bottom of the design is a contorted male figure plunging headfirst into a spiral vortex formed by the coils of a snake, which also describes a circle around the figure. Great flames burn on either side, and above these, at the left, is another contorted figure placed beneath the weighted balances, which doubtless refer to his fall.

With characteristic modesty, Alan Thomas sold the leaf as a probable posthumous impression struck by Mrs Catherine Blake's executor, the sculptor and miniaturist Frederick Tatham. But I, and others who have examined the leaf, are convinced that it was printed by Blake himself. The colour is a light sepia, a colour rarely used by Tatham, and the margins are wiped clean, a feature more common to proofs pulled by Blake than to those of Tatham.

On the back at the bottom right-hand corner is this inscription, lightly and neatly written in ink: 'J. Deffett Francis 1834', and at the top left-hand corner, in pencil and in a different, unidentified hand: 'This is a page from one/of Blake's books— perhaps/the America.'

John Deffett Francis (1815 or 1816-1901), a painter, was an early collector of Blake, among whose holdings were various pencil drawings and several plates from the illuminated books; many of the drawings he gave to the British Museum Print Room, and of the plates to Swansea Public Library. He also owned an early manuscript, called 'The Passions' by W.M. Rossetti, who acquired it in 1876 from Francis; it is now in the Berg Collection at New York Public Library.

The plates seem to have been acquired at about the same time as *America* plate 5, for at least one of them is similarly inscribed 'J. Deffett Francis 1834'. This was the year that Francis left his native Swansea to take up a career as a painter in London; he was then nineteen. He became acquainted with Frederick Tatham from whom he almost certainly acquired his Blake prints. Perhaps that is what gave rise to the idea that the present proof was pulled by Tatham; but it must be remembered that although Tatham took impressions from Blake's plates, he also inherited from Mrs Blake some of Blake's

Albions Angel stood beside the Stone
   of night, and saw
The terror like a comet, or more like the
   planet red
That once inclos'd the terrible wandering comets in its sphere.
Then Mars thou wast our center, & the planets three flew round
Thy crimson disk; so eer the Sun was rent from thy red sphere;
The Spectre glowd his horrid length staining the temple long
With beams of blood; & thus a voice came forth, and shook the
   temple

The Last Judgement, 304x245mm

Charles L. Dodgson
on the Authorized Version, Oxford, 1892

DECHERD TURNER

Humanities Research Center, University of Texas, Austin

Some years ago, Mr Alan Thomas furnished the Humanities Research Center, The University of Texas at Austin, a letter by Charles Dodgson which reflects in its content something of the contours of Mr Thomas's bookselling career and tastes. Most of the many Bibles Mr Thomas has sold have carried the wonderfully elevating cadence of the King James text. And then there is *Alice*, evocative of Mr Thomas's own subtle humour and compassion. These interests appear in the Reverend Dodgson's letter:

Ch. Ch. Oxford
Mar. 3 (92

Dear Sir,

I am reading your delightful book "The Living Christ & the four Gospels" with the greatest interest and profit. May I suggest how great a boon it would be, probably to a very large proportion of your readers, if you could issue an edition of it, in which the quotations should be from the *Authorised*, not the *Revised*, Version?

There must be hundreds, if not thousands, of probable readers of your book, who love the Authorised Version as familiar to them from childhood, and who simply *hate* (as I do) the New Version, with its wanton defacement of some of the loveliest passages in our dear old Bible.

Believe me
truly yours
(Rev.) Charles L. Dodgson

Rev. R.W. Dale

In the light of these perimeters, it seemed appropriate to us to convey our greetings and salutations in a visual and verbal way which would combine all portions of this rewarding combination:

C hevalier—	A lan—	A ll
H ail!—	L et—	U s
A pplaud—	A nd—	T oll in
R ising—	N ote—	H is
L aurels.—	T he—	O ccasion's
E ulogy—	H olds—	R estraint
S uspect.—	O des—	I ncite
D eclarations—	M ade—	Z ealous for
O ur—	A lan.—	E bullient
D on!—	S upremely—	D ynamic!
G ive—		T hanks
S aluting—	E ver—	E xceptional
O lympian—	S ocratic—	X enophonic
N oble—	Q uotable—	T homas

[Continued from page 68]

original proofs.

It is possible, too, that Francis acquired, perhaps indirectly, some of his other Blake items from Tatham's collection. Tatham disposed of the remainder of his Blake items in 1862, and many of them were bought by a Mr Harvey, who may have been a dealer and who probably sold them to Francis, for some of those given to the British Museum by Francis were listed as the property of Harvey by W.M. Rossetti in the first (1863) edition of Alexander Gilchrist's *Life of William Blake*.

Such are the fascinating byways to be explored following the acquisition of a William Blake leaf from Alan Thomas!

It is now safely mounted in a handmade paper frame and contained in a quarter morocco binding with marbled sides, the work of Sandy Cockerell. It may be examined back and front without being touched: if it is desired to examine the reverse, the binding is simply closed, turned over and opened from the back, a simple but ingenious solution to the problem of examining a leaf that could easily become tender if it were handled too much. The Fitzwilliam Museum recently had each leaf of Blake's manuscript of *An Island in the Moon* similarly mounted.

Ch. Ch. Oxford
Mar. 3/92

Dear Sir,

I am reading your delightful book "The Living Christ & the Four Gospels" with the greatest interest and profit. May I suggest how great a boon it would be, probably, to a very large proportion of your readers, if you could issue an edition of it, in which the quotations should be from the Authorised (not the Revised) Version?

There must be hundreds, if not thousands, of probable readers of your book, who love the Authorised Version (the Authorised Version as familiar to them from childhood), & who simply hate (as I do) the New Version, with its wanton defacement of some of the loveliest passages in our dear old Bible.

Believe me
Truly yours
(Rev.) Charles L. Dodgson

Rev. R. W. Dale

A letter from Charles Dodgson to R.W. Dale, Oxford, 3 March 1892

A Presentation Binding
London, 1981

BERNARD MIDDLETON

London

My wife, Dora, and I first met Alan about twenty-five years ago at his house in Bournemouth when we were taken there to meet him by the late Eric Burdett, a local binder and teacher, with whom we were staying for the weekend. I recall that we sat around in the famous 'Georgian' room, drank red wine, and talked about books, architecture, and many other subjects which interest this man who has such a huge appetite for life and experience. Since then, in the course of a friendly business relationship, during which his courtesy and patience have been unfailing, I have enjoyed the privilege of handling some of Alan's finest books and benefited from his illuminating comments, often made very casually, as the volumes were passed to me. The books have ranged from fine manuscripts of the fourteenth century to printed books of the nineteenth, and in between embraced many of the major landmarks in the history of printing and bookbinding.

Most of my work has involved restoration, or rebinding in period style when absolutely necessary, so I have welcomed this opportunity to produce a somewhat more modern binding for him, especially as this one is for his own library. 'Somewhat more' are the operative words as I am not noted for my adventurous avant-garde approach to design.

Time was an important factor, not only because it was necessary for me to decide at an early stage what to do so that the tooling pattern could be reproduced here, but there was the additional compli-cation that I was likely to be working in the United States in September and October at the time of the presentation of the bound copy of the book, thus appreciably reducing available working time after delivery of the sheets. Bearing this in mind I adopted a technique which involved onlaying gold-tooled leather into recesses in the leather-covered boards, which had the advantage that I could complete all the tooling, except that on the spine, even before the book was printed, instead of being forced to wait until I had bound and covered the book in the usual manner. The recesses were formed by cutting the circular shapes out of thin millboard and then making laminates with the main boards, which, incidentally, provides greater stability than is afforded by unlaminated boards. Many of my designs are closely related to the dimensions of the book, but as I could not be sure of these, or at least of the exact thickness of the text block, I thought it safer on this occasion to have a central motif.

The book is bound in bright red goatskin with green gold-tooled onlays and central black onlays tooled in palladium. The doublures are of black suede. For the flyleaves I had contemplated Japanese yellow paper with tufts of brown fibre embedded in it, but finally I decided that the dignity of light grey Fabriano Roma handmade paper with its handsome texture was more appropriate. The book has a ¼-red goat drop-back box with green cloth sides and black suede linings.

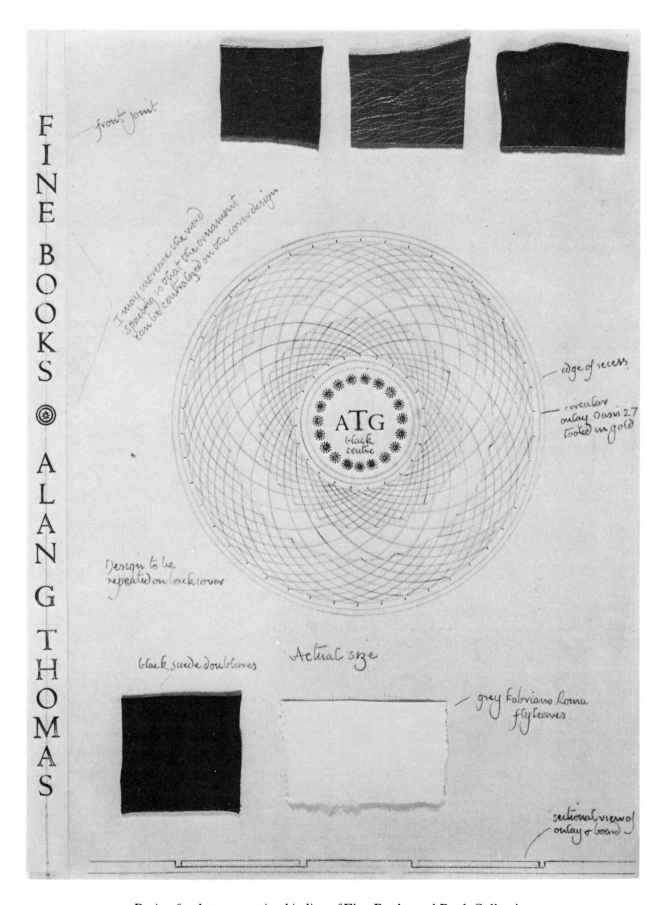

Design for the presentation binding of Fine Books and Book Collecting